BALANCING YOUR

FAMILY,

FAITH &

WORK

Wally —

May God Bless You!

BALANCING YOUR

FAMILY,

FAITH &

WORK

PAT GELSINGER

An imprint of
Cook Communications Ministries

Life Journey is an imprint of
Cook Communications Ministries, Colorado Springs, Colorado 80918
Cook Communications, Paris, Ontario
Kingsway Communications, Eastbourne, England

BALANCING YOUR FAMILY, FAITH & WORK

First Printing, 2003

Printed in the United States of America

1 2 3 4 5 6 7 8 9 10 Printing/Year 07 06 05 04 03

Editor: Larry Weeden; Sr. Editor, Craig Bubeck
Cover Design: M. C. D. Design

.

Library of Congress Cataloging-in-Publication Data

Gelsinger, Pat.

  Balancing family, faith, and work / by Pat Gelsinger.

      p. cm.

Includes bibliographical references.

  ISBN 0-7814-3899-3 (pbk.)

  1. Family--Religious life. 2. Work--Religious aspects--Christianity.

I. Title.

  BV4526.3.G45 2003

  248.4--dc21

                                                              2003008991

PREFACE:

This topic and book have as much to do with who I am and my life as they do with who my family members are and their lives. Thus I must acknowledge each one's life as it reflects into my own. While in many cases I am the visible face at work, at church, and in the leadership of our home, often the real substance and strength lie in the family that backs me up day and night. You might look at aspects of my life and be impressed, but the real heroes are a supportive wife and children who have been blessed by God and are a great blessing to me.

Of course, the greatest acknowledgment goes to my dear wife, Linda. At one anniversary, a wave of emotion came over me, causing me to pronounce regarding our relationship: "While it seems we were married just yesterday, it's like we've been together forever." In many ways, that defines our relationship, still fresh, new and powerful, yet it's hard to remember life before she came into my world. I've grown in compassion and affection for her as the years have proceeded.

Linda is the backbone of the Gelsinger household. As my travels take me to and fro on too many occasions, she more than holds the fort down on the home front. With a clear and certain view of what is right and what is wrong, she is ready to both encourage and challenge me when I get out of balance in any aspect of my life. While this may sound trite, it is more than true that this message and this book would never have been possible without her. To Linda, my Lady and Love, thank you.

The support, love, and affection of our children bring me both joy and delight. To Elizabeth, thank you for being a young Christian woman demonstrating God's character in your daily life. While I've appreciated the times I've been able to teach you, you've taught me much and brought me even greater joy in return. How I enjoy watching God transform you from girl to teen to woman. He will use you and your desire to be an elementary teacher in powerful ways as you remain committed to let him be the God of your life.

Josiah, I enjoy your quick thinking and intelligence. Watching you grow to adulthood is both exciting and frightening. Every game I watch you play makes me proud to be your father. You are racing to manhood too quickly and how wonderful to see God prepare you to be a man. Thank you for challenging me both to be home and to be really home when I am there.

Nathan, how refreshing is your seemingly perpetual joy and enthusiasm for life. I cannot describe the pleasure of seeing so many characteristics of my own being lived again in you. I look forward to watching how God will work in your life as you follow his call for your life to enter full-time ministry. Thank you for making our home forever exciting, interesting, and always unique.

To Micah, thank you for your determination and dogged pursuit of what is right and true. While our youngest is too soon to burst into the teenage years, you will forever be my little boy. Thank you for your love and your joy of being with me and doing just about anything I'm doing. May your dream of being a missionary to Kenya become true as you grow in maturity in the Lord.

Finally, I thank Bryce Jessup, our pastor for many years, the man who married Linda and I, a mentor and a friend. Also, you are one I've been able to mentor and encourage to "not be a wimp" when considering how big our God really is. More than any other, you've encouraged—no, demanded—I write this text. Thank you for editing, commenting, and constantly emailing me the message, "that's good, add it to your book." I look forward to continued years of encouragement and mentoring, and maybe the second revision will even more reflect your great wisdom poured into my life. Most of all, thank you for being a friend and brother in Christ.

INTRODUCTION

I have given this message in speech form to many men's groups, business groups, and gatherings of professionals across the United States. I've presented it in India, Taiwan, mainland China, Germany, Singapore, Hong Kong, and Japan. The response has been overwhelmingly positive. Somehow this message has found a resonance in the lives of audience members. Our world today is increasingly busy, and it appears that men and women in the rat race, .com craze, the home vs. business trap, workaholics, and many others are crying out for some way to manage the increasing busyness and craziness of our times. I've heard it said that Satan doesn't need to deceive us, he just needs to keep us busy. All that busyness, of course, can lead to an ineffective witness, career struggles, family strife, divorce, and ultimate failure in one's personal and professional lives.

During our family's summer vacation in 1999, I read the book *Half Time*, by Bob Buford[1], which has a simple and powerful message: From Success to Significance. If you haven't read that work yet, I highly recommend it. Read it through when you have a bit of time to ponder your life and career. As we've labored through a significant portion of our time on earth, what are we seeking? The next rung of the ladder toward career success? The next material acquisition that declares success to our friends and neighborhood? Maybe the acceptance letter for our children at the top name school? Some other form of worldly recognition?

Buford's book is good and yet terrible to read on a vacation. Instead of the mindless relaxation I was planning during vacation, it challenged me to a period of deep self-reflection and consideration of my life's purpose. As I analyzed myself, I, too, confronted the question of whether I was investing my life in the right things. Was I out for success or significance? Should I consider a dramatic restructuring of my life, as Buford had done? Should I step out of the corporate world entirely and simply "be home" to focus single-mindedly on my family?

I had seen powerfully, early in my life, that my career and position at Intel were exactly where God wanted me to be. Thus, while the idea of getting out of the rat race and the challenge of juggling life was attractive, and I had been so blessed financially that I could seriously consider saying to the CEO of Intel, "I'll give you a call in ten years when the kids are all graduated." However, that wasn't God's purpose for me at the time. Instead, I was sensing this increasingly enthusiastic response to the message of my life. God wanted to use me in my position at Intel and what I had learned as a juggler of time and priorities to influence others for his kingdom.

After speaking at a Timeout conference in the fall of 2000 on this subject, I was challenged by a number of the participants to write a book. One in particular said, "I have heard no one with as much to say as you do who hasn't written it down."

As my busy, juggling lifestyle had plenty of demands already, I was reluctant to undertake this project. Having co-authored a book once before, *Programming the 80386*[2] (great for the nightstand, it will surely send you off to a good night's sleep), I was well acquainted with the amount of work involved in writing a quality book.

However, after numerous individuals encouraged me in this regard, I decided to give it a shot. In the spare minutes, late hours, and long plane flights to and fro, I began to write. In fact, I undertook the writing process without conferring with Linda. I knew she'd be uncomfortable with another project and determined to finish a draft in my spare time to assure it wouldn't be yet another burden on the family. She was, to say the least, startled when I proclaimed a completed first draft.

During my once-every-seven-year sabbatical from Intel, I found enough spare time to get a near-final work. Just this one last trip to Asia and it was now ready to give to the publisher. My prayer is that you might find this book useful in your personal juggling act. If just a few of you who read this find one or two of my suggestions of any utility, the many hours of typing will be more than justified.

The book is broken into seven main chapters. The first is, simply, my testimony. As I've delivered this message as a lecture, I've found that when people hear my story, the points of the remaining chapters take on greater meaning and clarity. Often people will make comments like, "If you can do that, certainly I can manage in my situation." You'll soon see that I've been extraordinarily blessed through a series of what some would call coincidences. But I see them as blessings from the divine Creator and Overseer of the universe. As my father would say, "I'm not sure why I've been chosen to be so blessed, but I have been." While I fear a testimony of such overwhelming blessing might come through as pride, it is what God has done in my life.

Hopefully, through it you might learn just a bit about who I am, who my wife and family are, what I've accomplished at Intel and in our church, and what God has done in each of these areas of my life.

Chapters 2 through 7 lay out six specific principles for becoming a master juggler of life's priorities. Each principle is illustrated by examples from my life, and each chapter ends with several questions to help you apply this material to your own life or possibly in a group setting.

I'm a Christian. As a born-again believer in the Lord Jesus Christ, my faith is at the foundation of who I am, what I stand for, what I dream of accomplishing, and what I desire to become as a man. My faith is an inextricable element of my personality and my life's experiences. I write from a Christian perspective and make no apologies for my faith. I couldn't write a book of this sort and not reflect my faith in a central and substantive manner.

With that in mind, however, I recognize that some, hopefully many, who read this book may not share my faith. I believe this book can still be of utility to you. In particular, chapters 3 through 6 can be applied wholly and with little hesitation regardless. You might find chapters 1, 2, and 7 a bit arduous. While I don't apologize for who I am in these areas of the book, I do hope you'll still find them interesting. Of course, my greatest joy would be that through my testimony you also might choose to trust and serve the risen Savior, Jesus Christ.

CONTENTS

CHAPTER 1

Testimony

I was born and raised in Robesonia, Pennsylvania. This is in Pennsylvania Dutch country just outside Reading, the outlet capital of the USA. Both of my parents' families were farmers. My mother was from a family of eleven, with many of her siblings never making it past infancy. My dad was from a family of nine children. He was a twin at number seven in the family. With pride he tells his sister Mary, "I came out first." Both Mom and Dad were of Pennsylvania Dutch upbringing, learning English as their second language. While they grew up some sixty miles apart, each walked to their nearest one-room schoolhouse for their first through eighth grade education. Neither was given the opportunity to pursue a higher education beyond eighth grade. For both of my parents, their large families made up a high percentage of the student body in the tiny one-room schoolhouse.

As each of my dad's siblings reached the age of maturity and marriage, they moved into farming with a bit of financial assistance from Grandpa. Grandpa helped son #1, son #2, daughter #1 etc., but when finally getting to my dad as the seventh child, he said, "You're on your own, son." Thus, my father began his farming career working with his brothers.

There's always more than enough work to do on a farm. Thus, Dad was more than welcome to work with a couple of my uncles. This worked wonderfully until cousins started to get to the age of maturity and Dad became less central to the operations of my uncles' farms. On several occasions Dad looked into buying a farm, but he was never quite the high bidder or the loan didn't quite go through. Thus, he never did acquire a farm of his own.

I enjoyed the hard work of the farm, and I always liked working with Dad. Had Dad ever acquired a farm of his own, I'd be there to this day, working with him on the family homestead.

I learned much from my dad and my farming uncles, aunts, and cousins. It's hard to be closely associated with this environment and not develop a deep and powerful work ethic. Up early every day, hard manual labor from dawn to dusk and late to bed being totally exhausted from a hard day's labor.

While Dad worked on the farm with my uncles, he also took on a position in the local steel mill and finally was a Township supervisor overseeing most of their road building and maintenance. For almost all my formative years I saw him working three jobs simultaneously. He worked hard to provide a lifestyle and environment for his family that was better than the one he was raised in. To this day, I consider myself somewhat lazy compared to him. In many ways, he's one of the heroes of my life.

I can recall more than one instance where one of my uncles or the owner of the horse farm where I worked for several years would reprove me for errors in my character or weaknesses in my work ethic. My Uncle Edwin put me to work when I was barely able to lift a hay bale. One day my Uncle Lester saw one of the young men I was hanging around with and made clear to me that this individual's influence on me would not be positive. On another occasion, after working for an entire week for my Uncle Clarence, payday came. I recall when he paid me for my labors with a $50 bill. At the time, this was nigh unto a fortune (at least in my eyes). I think he wisely knew I'd be reluctant to break the $50 bill and thus, would be far less likely to allow those newfound funds to burn a hole in my pocket. Instead of quickly running out and spending them, I flashed that $50 bill for weeks to all my friends and family as if it were a bar of gold.

We attended church every Sunday. My family and much of my immediate relatives attended the United Church of Christ in nearby Wernersville. I was baptized at six days old and only missed a Sunday under rare circumstances of illness. We polished our shoes Saturday night, got up Sunday morning, put on our jackets and ties, and went to church. Dad disliked being late for church, so we rarely were. This was just the way it was, and I was not about to disrupt the family's routine.

I was formally confirmed when I was twelve years old. This was the process by which one became a full member of the congregation. I became president of the youth group at fourteen. By all outward appearances, I was a shining example of a Christian young man. I was at church every Sunday, knew the hymns well, did my turn as altar boy, and was president of the youth group. What else could you want or expect from a guy? Some years later when my wife-to-be, Linda, asked if I was a Christian, the reply without hesitation or doubt was: yes! And I proceeded to recite this same list of evidences why that assertion was true.

But the reality of my life was far different. While I was a perfect specimen on Sundays, the remainder of the week was another story. By the time I was seventeen I had experimented with many of the temptations of our age. Several of the guys I hung around with were not the kind of company you would want for friends of your children.

Living a lie was fun, daring, and challenging. I liked being seen as the perfect boy. Every mother and grandmother would compliment me and convey their desire for me to be their own each Sunday.

My life was like those coin bins that sit at the doorways of some diners and restaurants. You drop a coin in the top and it goes spiraling slowly downward. While the coin might think the ride is wonderful, thrilling, and fun, the end point is absolute and final; it lands in the hole at the bottom 100 percent of the time—there is no exception to the law of gravity. For those in such a lifestyle as I was, the end is equally final—a hole at the end of life called hell. That's the path I was on, and I was making good time.

God had blessed me with a good mind, however, and He began to use it to steer me in a different direction. Having determined I probably wasn't going to be a farmer (since my Dad had never purchased his own farm), I considered a variety of alternatives and decided upon electronics. Partially out of typical high school boredom, and partially out of interest in electronics, I began attending Berks Vocational Technical School in the afternoons of my sophomore and junior years. The teacher of the class, Howard Buck, was particularly encouraging to me. He challenged my lifestyle on more than one occasion, seeing both my capability as well as my decaying lifestyle and friendships. It was during this time that I accidentally took the Lincoln Technical Institute's electronics technology scholarship exam (the test was supposed to be for seniors, but I won a full two-year scholarship as a junior).

This posed a certain difficulty. I wasn't yet a senior and wouldn't be graduating from high school for another year and a half. However, the scholarship was only offered for the following school year. Thus, a chapter of my life began to unfold that I would have never anticipated. I was somewhat bored with high school, and a change of pace seemed intriguing. To a young man who was increasingly enamored by a worldly lifestyle, the prospect of increased freedom was attractive as well.

With a scholarship and greater challenges in front of me, I skipped my last year of high school and began working toward my Associates Degree at Lincoln Technical Institute at the ripe old age of seventeen. After commuting for a few months, and after being in a car accident, my parents and I decided to move me into an apartment immediately adjacent to the school. While my roommates were generally nice guys, they were also worldly and active in drinking, drugs, and rock-n-roll. Now with a daughter who has passed through the age of seventeen, I can't believe I left home at that early age. But while I don't recommend people rush into life as quickly as I did, God was clearly working my poor choices toward good. He was about to begin a mighty and amazing work in me.

Not only did I start working on my two-year degree at seventeen, but I also accelerated my coursework at Lincoln Tech. Instead of taking six quarters, I doubled up one quarter and finished in five. I needed some basic math, English, and history courses for high school graduation too, and I took those at night at our local Lehigh Valley Community College. As you'll see further along, I was intense and disciplined. Given my farming background, I was comfortable working hard, and I generally do well on about five hours of sleep.

During this period, I also began part-time work. While my classes were paid for by my scholarship, I needed money for rent, gas, and books. The local radio and TV station, WFMZ, hired me mostly to do equipment maintenance and repair, but I also managed to get a few weekend night shifts of keeping music on the air and running the TV programs. After doubling on classes, taking evening classes, and now working evenings and weekends, my skills for a career as a juggler were already getting underway.

At Lincoln Tech I had my first experience with computers. To this point I had been intrigued with electronics in general. With my position at WFMZ, I was mostly looking at analog technologies used in broadcasting and communications. But after playing with my first computer, I was hooked. I knew what I wanted to do with the rest of my career the day after I first used one. I began playing with a Radio Shack TRS 80, my first RSA 1802, and other simple training computers Lincoln had available. While I was enthusiastic about electronics in general, computers became my passion. I consumed everything I could find on the subject.

In my last quarter of Lincoln I began to interview for electronics technician positions. I interviewed with a variety of East Coast companies like IBM and Western Electric. I also decided to talk with a West Coast company named Intel, which had come recruiting for technicians. Generally, Intel didn't recruit in the East, but they were growing rapidly and there was an industry wide shortage of technicians. I was the last interviewee in what had been a long day (packed with twelve candidates) for Ron J. Smith, an engineering manager for Intel at the time. His reactions were reflected in the brief summary he wrote about me: "somewhat arrogant, very aggressive and smart—he'll fit right in."

To this day, Ron and I remain friends and coworkers. His parents live close to mine, and we humorously reflect on Pennsylvania stories and our early interactions. Whenever I do something he doesn't like at Intel, I tell him it's his own fault—he recruited me.

From this interview, I received an invitation to visit Intel. I was eighteen years old and had never been on an airplane beyond the Appalachian Mountains. Now I could have a free trip to the growing and already famous Silicon Valley of Californiaaa (say the "a" long and slow, to get the right effect). After careful and thoughtful consideration that lasted about two nanoseconds, I accepted the invitation to visit California (uh, I mean, uh, Intel). However, before departing I assured my mother, "Don't worry, Mom, no way am I moving all the way to the West Coast—I'm an East Coast boy."

While I was off on my interview trip to California, my mother was having major surgery. On the day of my return, I walked into her hospital room, and the instant she saw me, she knew. I was bound for the wild west. Despite my earlier assurances to her, the West had now captured my interest. In one of several marvelous, divine coincidences in my life, this was the only year that Intel ever came recruiting at Lincoln Tech. Had I not "accidentally" taken that scholarship exam, I'd never have had the opportunity to interview with Intel.

I thus graduated with my high school class in June 1979, finished my Associates degree at the top of my class in August 1979 from

Lincoln Tech, and left for California in October 1979 to start working at Intel. It had been an amazing a year.

Off to California

My relatives were full of encouragement for my moving to California: "Earthquakes will make California fall into the ocean." "California girls will love you and leave you." "Everyone's a beach bum there." "Watch out for all those cults." I became a black sheep of some significance as I moved to the other side of the country.

I recall my first day driving into Santa Clara and sitting at the intersection of El Camino Real and San Thomas Expressway. On my left was a low-rider bouncing up and down. (If you're not familiar with this modified contraption of a car, you gotta see one to even believe they exist.) On my right was a souped up car with the bass playing so loudly it made my car vibrate. When the light turned green, I was about to go when three cars went racing through the intersection in front of me. I did a U-turn at the next intersection, made my way to a corner seat in a nearby restaurant, had a cup of coffee, and began wondering what on earth I was doing there—this place was crazy.

That was just the beginning. A few days after I began work at Intel I was sitting in a training session for new hires when the instructor shrieked, "Earthquake, under the tables!" I left skid marks on the carpet, I hit the ground so fast. That evening I was sitting at home, studying at the kitchen table, when an aftershock hit. I was so startled I jumped backward over the chair and landed like a cat in the middle of the room. At least in Pennsylvania the earth didn't shake. Had I had the money or a plane ticket at the time, I would have used it to flee to the comfortable surroundings of my hometown. I believe this was one of the ways God was preparing me for some dramatic changes in my life. Before I was ready to make such changes, He was preparing me to see both my inadequacies and the ultimate results of my current lifestyle.

I knew no one in California except for a couple of guys who came from Lincoln Tech and took jobs at Intel at the same time I did. Thus, the suggestion to get a house together was easy to accept. While my salary seemed like a fortune for an East Coast farm boy, I quickly found that living in California was expensive, and I could not even come close to affording an apartment of my own. Furthermore, having someone familiar around was comforting for this 18-year-old far from home.

Jack was a guitar playing, pot smoking, drug using, hot-rodding, rock-n-roller. Bob was a neo-Nazi kind of guy who collected guns, grenades, and bomb materials. As you might expect, spirituality wasn't a strong point of our bachelor trio home.

As noted earlier, I was in church each Sunday from my infancy. However, shortly after arriving in California, Jack encouraged me to repaint my 1966 Chevy Belair. It was worse than a sight for sore eyes. It was originally a sort of blue-green color, but after an accident my Dad and I replaced the front fenders and hood with a blue front end from a 1965 Impala. Add to this a bit of rust and some body patch on the rear quarter panels, and voila, quite a sight it was. Jack was experienced in painting cars, and—I think—desperate to avoid the public disgrace of his roommate's eyesore parked in the driveway. So we undertook a paint job.

Thus, with my car out of commission, for that first weekend living in California I decided to walk to the nearest church rather than seeking out a UCC church that would have been true to my roots. It was Santa Clara Christian Church just a few blocks down the street.

At the end of the first service I attended there, two girls, Karen and Linda, came up to greet this young visitor. They seemed a bit giggly, but were friendly (as one is supposed to be to visitors). When I identified myself as having just moved to California and started with Intel, Linda immediately asked, "Do you eat in the cafeteria?" This question struck me as odd for a first question to ask someone you are welcoming to church, and in response I gave her a perplexed look. This expression sent the two of them off giggling.

Well, a couple of silly high school girls had absolutely zero appeal to me. It turns out that she worked for the food services company that ran the cafeterias at Intel, so her seemingly odd question wasn't really silly, but it certainly did start us off on the wrong foot.

Linda didn't find me any more appealing than I found her. She looked at me as a smart aleck kid, while she was several years older and far more mature. We couldn't have been further from love at first sight.

It was another one of those divine coincidences—only a couple of weeks later, when my car would be back in driving condition, I probably never would have chosen to attend this church. Instead, I would have gone looking for something closer to my denominational heritage. However, as I became involved with the youth group activities, this young lady was almost always there. Thus, Linda and I began to strike up an acquaintance.

While my roommates and I were quite the bachelors and not particularly domesticated, we decided to have a Thanksgiving feast for our few friends in the area. I invited Linda over to join us. After the meal and clean-up, we went for a nice walk around the neighborhood and discussed a wide range of personal and spiritual topics.

Upon our return from our walk, we entered the house through the living room, where Jack, Bob, and some of the other guests were gathered around a strange contraption emitting a funny odor. Linda and I went into the other room and were talking and looking at pictures. She asked what they were doing out there. I replied nonchalantly, "They're smoking pot in a bong."

Linda was aghast. "If the police came right now, they'd throw me in jail!" she exclaimed. She refused to ever come back to the house and began to strongly encourage me to seek new roommates.

She also started taking this young man Pat before the Lord in earnest, and she got several prayer warriors at the Santa Clara Church to join her in praying me out of this den of iniquity—fast! This was just the beginning of her prayer journey for this smart aleck kid from Pennsylvania.

As I began to regularly attend Santa Clara Church and became involved with the youth group, I grew increasingly convicted about my other six-days-of-the-week lifestyle. You see, the UCC church I grew up in, as many of the mainline denominations of today have sadly become, was a pleasant place to be. The sermons made you feel good and generally encouraged you to live a better life. They held fine social events. There are many fine Christians in these churches, as there were in my hometown church. However, the church didn't emphasize teaching the gospel, developing a personal relationship with Christ, convicting one of sin and its consequences, and demanding a New Testament lifestyle. As I began to see the gospel unfold in front of my eyes, I was aware that my lifestyle was increasingly far off the mark. While I had believed myself to be a Christian and declared such to Linda and many others, I had no personal relationship with and faith in Jesus Christ.

In February 1980, Gary Fraley, the minister at Santa Clara at the time, gave a sermon using Revelation 3:15 as the text.

"I know your deeds, that you are neither cold nor hot. I wish you were either one or the other! So, because you are lukewarm—neither hot nor cold—I am about to spit you out of my mouth" (Rev. 3:15-16).

From this I could clearly see that my other six days of the week lifestyle placed me in the lukewarm category at best. I was, as Revelation so boldly declared, ready to be spit out of the mouth of the Lord.

As I've since studied the book of Revelation more deeply, this is a horrifyingly graphic picture. What could be more detestable an image than comparing one's self or life to spit or vomit? There are few more grotesque images presented in the entirety of the Bible.

With this conviction upon my heart I made that step of faith, claiming Jesus as my Lord and Savior, understanding and repenting of my sins, turning toward a new way of life, and finally being baptized through the waters symbolizing his death, burial and resurrection. I became a new creation in him. February 1980 was my second birth, my spiritual birthday. All of a sudden a new life and lifestyle began to unfold.

One day the week after my new birth, I was casually walking down the hallway in Intel's Santa Clara 4 building. As I made a typical stroll on the way to the cafeteria, this man came up to me who was on the short but fit side. He was clean shaven, dark hair, wearing glasses and probably around thirty years old. I had never met him before and didn't have any reason to believe he knew me. As he walked closer to me, he was clearly seeking my attention, and apparently wanting to have a discreet conversation. "Greetings, I'm Bob Matthews," he said. We shook hands, and I was struck by his politeness and expected him to discuss some work related topic. But then he quickly informed me that God had led him to be my roommate.

I was shocked. God led him? How bizarre. How weird! God was communicating to him about me? This was like one of those supernatural apocalyptic movies that were popular at the time. God doesn't just lead people, especially not when it's about me! While peculiar and unnerving, it was also clear my current rock-n-roll and neo-Nazi roommates were not the spiritual environment I needed as a baby Christian. Bob was a mature Christian, a quiet and helpful man, and just about perfect for me at the time. This leading from God was an example of his personally directing my life. As I was working and going to school and spending most every free moment in study, God had—in another of those divine coincidences—provided the perfect roommate.

The prayers of Linda and the other prayer warriors were answered; a new roommate and a spiritually encouraging environment were provided by God. With my newfound faith in the Lord Jesus Christ, the first of the great changes in my life in California was complete.

School

My first boss at Intel was David A. Brown, who had gone to great lengths to comfort my parents. In fact, before I had even left the East Coast, David had talked with my parents several times assuring them that "it would be okay" and "I'll make sure he is fine" when their young son moved to California. Intel was a great employer, and I had a position in the Q+A group of the microprocessor department.

On my first day of work, Dave explained the things he needed me to do for him. He was running a variety of quality and reliability experiments and he needed me to load chips into ovens, run some tests on them at periodic intervals, verify the functioning of the test board and its load of chips, and then reload them into the ovens for additional stresses and tests. While not the entirety of my responsibilities, this was a large part of my starting assignment.

As I sat there listening to him, my singular career goal quickly congealed in my mind, I wanted to be on the other side of the table. I wanted to be the one deciding the experiments, interpreting the data, and giving the directions—the engineer who decided what to do, not the technician who did the grunt work. That was the sum total of my career objectives at the time—to be an engineer.

From this humble beginning, my career was underway. I spent all my spare hours working. I loved it. When I wasn't busy with school, I'd easily work eighty or ninety hours in a week; often breaking the bank on overtime pay for our department. A couple of times my overtime was so extensive that payroll complained. I just told them to pay me for whatever number of hours didn't cause a problem. If you are enjoying what you do, do they need to pay you for it?

One of the main reasons I had accepted a position with Intel was to continue my education. Now, it was quickly becoming clear that I wanted to be an engineer and proceed to graduate level studies as well. Of the many job offers I had received, Intel offered me by far the most flexible work schedule, and any full-time employee who took a work-related course and received a grade of B would be fully reimbursed by the company.

With this policy and an agreement from my boss to allow me flexible work hours, I began my full-time studies at Santa Clara University in March 1980. I continued diligently for three years to complete my BS in Electrical Engineering. Then I immediately enrolled at Stanford University, where I earned my master's in June '85. Following that, I spent another year getting started on my Ph.D. at Stanford. Based on Intel's reimbursement policy (which required working 30 hours per week) I was underway with the cheapest expensive education one could ever have. Though I stopped attending school fifteen years ago, I believe I still hold the record for the amount of tuition reimbursement at Intel.

With this intense schedule of full-time work and full-time school, I took my next step toward becoming a first class juggler. I worked anywhere from 30-80 hours per week depending on my school load. For over six years I took either 12-18 credits a quarter at SCU or 8-10 master's level credits at Stanford. During this period I became well acquainted with living on 4-5 hours of sleep per night, thankful for the high energy level God had given me. I would typically get up at 6:30 A.M. for my first class at 8:00. Then I'd work at Intel through the afternoon and evening, ending with study till 1:00 or 2:00 A.M. I became extraordinarily self-disciplined in my use of the most precious resource that God gives to each of us—time.

Having come from a small technical school on the East Coast, I was somewhat intimidated in my first quarter at Santa Clara University. Everyone here was smarter than anything I'd experienced before. I was frightened knowing that if I didn't get a B or better, Intel wasn't going to reimburse me. I couldn't afford to pay for the classes myself. So I labored hard to earn good grades, studying every spare moment of my nights and weekends. After the first quarter I was getting As in all my classes, and I realized that with hard work I had a shot at being the top of the class. Thus, while it required great focus and increased diligence, I made up my mind to become class valedictorian.

With school and my career at Intel underway, the second of the great changes of my life in California was in full swing.

Linda

Having just moved to California in October 1979, I had neither funds nor vacation time for a trip home when Christmas came just a few months later. At the same time, Linda's father was out of town. Thus, Linda and her family had a major hole in their normal Christmas plans. They decided to take pity on this poor lonely boy from Pennsylvania.

I was invited to join Linda, her mother, Shirley, and her grandmother for a Christmas Eve meal. A bachelor far from home is seldom known to turn down a free meal, particularly when three generations of fine cooks were sharing the kitchen. Even though I wasn't all that interested in young Linda Sue at the time, the worst that could happen was that I wouldn't be quite so lonely, and I'd scarf a good meal in the process.

The evening exceeded everyone's expectations. We enjoyed a fine meal and good conversation and played a variety of games. I hit it off extremely well with Linda's grandmother. As we played cards, it seemed we had something akin to mental telepathy working between us. As partners, the other person always seemed to play just the right card or make the perfect move. The evening was wonderful, but I finally made a graceful departure for my apartment.

As Linda's grandmother closed the door behind me, she immediately turned and looked Linda in the eye. With generations of godly wisdom she declared to Linda and Shirley: "he's the one."

Linda not only didn't agree, but she was aghast at the suggestion. "Grandma, he's just eighteen years old," she protested. "I don't know him, and he's just a friend!"

Despite Linda's objections, Grandma Christensen was firm in her prophetic assertion. Linda had a great respect for her godly grandmother, and, almost, a fear that she saw something that she herself didn't yet understand about me. As Linda and I began seeing each other (casually but more regularly), her mother added to Linda's angst by reinforcing Grandma's opinion with her own: "he's the one." With both Mom and Grandma now rooting for me, you'd think I was certain to win over Linda. It just took her about two more years to be convinced.

As we began dating more and more, Linda quickly learned how my life was prioritized and organized. Between Intel and school I fit her in each Friday night for our date night. I needed a break from studies and work, and Friday night was it. Further, she almost always cooked me a fine Friday night dinner at her apartment. She would question—why don't we go out to eat? To which I'd reply, "But I love your home-cooked meals!" She could never quite tell if I was honest about her cooking or, just too cheap to take her out to eat. Both were true.

In addition to our Friday night dates, we'd see each other on Sundays at church. She would often cook a meal for us on Sunday afternoon. Then I'd hunch over my books at her apartment for several hours of studying while Linda would often curl up for a treat she'd look forward to all week—a Sunday afternoon nap. We'd then venture off to Sunday evening church service before bidding each other farewell until the next weekend. I'd call her almost every day during the week for a short conversation, but that was about it. Often the calls were nothing more than "don't have time but wanted to check in and make sure you knew I was thinking of you." Years later we would joke about this period saying, "we squeezed a year's worth of dating into three years."

On one occasion, Linda called me on Thursday and asked if we could get together. She'd had a disagreement and wanted someone to talk to. Being the flexible and nice guy I was, I said sure, no exams tomorrow and nothing due that I don't have finished. I spent a fair amount of time that evening discussing with her the situation between her and her dad. After a while together and discussing the complete situation, she was feeling better.

As I left that night Linda asked what we would do tomorrow, Friday night, our normal date night. I immediately responded, "Sorry, you had your night, I have to study tomorrow." She was shocked, angry, and terribly disappointed with me. All her girlfriends were see-ing their boyfriends four, five, or six days of the week, and now I was depriving her of the one night of the week I could squeak out for her. No date night! How could I be so cruel and callous? This led her to question if she could ever marry this guy. Would he ever change? Or would he always be so busy that he would never have time to fit her into his already full life? At a minimum, she'd think twice before ask-ing for my time on a different night of the week.

I had clear goals of finishing my bachelor's degree, my master's and finally my Ph.D. before even considering matrimony, and my family agreed. My mother, in particular, would often encourage me to continue my studies and finish my degrees. After I was promoted to be Intel's CTO (Chief Technology Officer), Mom's second question (after asking what a CTO was), predictably, was "When are you going to finish your Ph.D.?" Thus, while I was becoming increasingly fond of Linda, I had also made my intentions abundantly clear to her. While she might not have liked them, she didn't press the issue with me. Then, however, God began to work again.

Linda had a disease, endometriosis, which she had struggled with for a few years. Over many years of battling it, her reproductive organs had severely deteriorated. After we had been dating for a year and a half she had a surgery to correct some problems. She had many cysts that had grown on her ovaries, tubes, and uterus. One ovary was entirely removed, and part of the second ovary had to be removed as well. Following the surgery her gynecologist asked her if she was considering marriage? engaged? or maybe a boyfriend? She made it clear that, if she was to ever have any children, it needed to be soon—very soon. Despite Linda's reluctance, her doctor insisted that Linda needed to discuss her medical condition with her boyfriend.

Well, in June 1981 Linda had me come to her apartment, which wasn't grossly abnormal but somewhat atypical. She made clear to me ahead of time that she had some things she needed to discuss with me. When she came out with a foot-high stack of medical books, I knew I was in serious trouble. As she opened them up to the reproductive section, I had an eerie premonition. I was pretty certain I wasn't ready for whatever she was about to share.

As she opened them up she began explaining to me everything the surgery had done and everything the doctor had said to her. I was overwhelmed and confused. School was going well. I was nicely maturing in my infant Christian faith. Work was great. I was enjoying this casual dating relationship with Linda. Now . . .

My mind buzzed with each word as she pointed to various pictures. She was trying her best not to lose her composure as she systematically gave me the explanations of what the doctor and her own studies had brought her to understand about her condition. When she made the point about children now, or never, it stung like being hit with ice cold water while in a warm shower.

After she finished, I not only felt confused, but trapped as well. At this point, I had probably fallen in love with her. However, I couldn't just deprive her of any hope of natural motherhood. Should I simply break off the relationship and wish her well to find someone who didn't have a firm and clear plan such as I did? Could I reconsider my well laid plans that all seemed to be working perfectly to this point? I needed to think, pray, and consider what we'd discussed.

Thus, partially out of fear and motivated to just get away from the immediate conversation, I told her I'd give her an answer before school began in the fall. With that, the conversation was concluded, and I was more than anxious to get out of there. Marriage? Pregnancy? Children? I wanted a large family, maybe eight or twelve kids—but certainly not now. What are you trying to tell me, God?

I struggled all summer over this matter. We continued dating, but she could tell I was very troubled. Our times together were often just miserable. We spent a weekend camping with some dear friends, Joe and Kathy. As my school and work schedule was so busy, this was a good time to think and consider our relationship. It proved to be a wretched weekend, however, as Linda lived in constant fear that at any moment I'd blurt out that I'd decided to end our relationship.

After months of pondering and prayer, I did reach a decision. The last weekend before school started, I took her out to eat—it wasn't even a Friday night. Since I was pretty much a tightwad, taking her to her favorite fish restaurant was a pretty big deal.

I encouraged her to pick anything from the menu she wanted, anything at all. From Mr. Tightwad to Mr. Bighearted and Generous, she knew something was up—I even allowed for fresh whole lobster! By this point, her stomach was in such knots that she could barely eat. Still being very much a bachelor, I ate most of her portion as well.

When we went to my apartment after dinner, I had a dozen red roses awaiting her. Then, having finally listened to God's leading, I asked if she would be mine. With tears filling her eyes, she found the words and voice to say a clear and strong yes.

While I couldn't anticipate at the time how great a complement Linda would be for me, she certainly was and is God's perfect choice. As the years have progressed, I've been continually thrilled to see her open up like a rose in front of me, each petal holding another character quality or personality attribute that I had not known she possessed before. As each unfolds it almost miraculously complements me or answers the needs of the situation.

Where I'm extremely logical, she is emotional. While I might see the physical needs of the situation, she is sensitive to the emotional needs. I tend to be a maniac, forever trying to squeeze more into every week or day or hour. She understands how to rest and relax and acts like brakes on me, preventing me from spiraling out of control. Where I tend to react quickly and sometimes impulsively, she is much more methodical and practical. While leaving some things gray and ambiguous is just fine with me, she needs them to be perfectly black or white and insists on the highest clarity and integrity in everything. Being on time for me is plus or usually minus ten or fifteen minutes. For Linda, anything less than five minutes early is late. While I might be lax with what the kids watch or do, she is thorough, assuring our children are raised in a Christian and moral environment at all times.

While her doctor recommended marriage and pregnancy as quickly as possible, we decided to wait till the following summer to wed. We would plan it carefully, invite our relatives and go through marriage counseling at our church. While we were ready to wed and begin our family, we trusted that if God would give us children, he'd still provide them to us if we trusted him, waited till the following summer, and didn't try to rush into things.

As we approached our wedding day in August 1982, her doctor realized she hadn't been inoculated for Rubella. After receiving the shot right before the wedding, she wasn't to become pregnant for three months. At precisely three months of marriage, that remaining portion of her single ovary and her tattered reproductive organs conceived our first child. When she went to see her doctor, they both cried. The doctor, a female, said, "I can't believe it, I know what you look like inside." Remembering the barren womb of Elizabeth and her husband Zechariah, the parents of John the Baptist, we named our first child Elizabeth. Just as God had blessed Elizabeth and Zechariah with a miraculous pregnancy, so he had blessed us with a pregnancy that her doctor considered a miracle.

August 1982 was the summer before my senior year at Santa Clara University. I still had another year there and then grad school. Still being focused on my goal of being top of my class, I either hunkered over my desk each evening, studying away, worked late at Intel, or attended classes. I also studied all weekend long for most every week-end. While some might have thought the situation was terrible, Linda thought it was great. Instead of seeing me only on Friday night and at church on Sunday, she was seeing me every day and night. Even if she heard only a few words from me and watched me lean over my desk with my nose in a pile of technical books, we were at least together.

Imagine a person juggling three balls about the size of tennis balls. One of those balls represents God, one represents Family and the third represents Work. That's what my life felt like; I was constantly trying to keep all those balls in the air. I got no opportunity to pause, rest, or take a break. If I tired for a split second, one or more of the balls would go tumbling to the ground.

Of course, you never really finish with a ball. You just prioritize it (catch it) and spend some time working/helping/doing with it (holding it), and then you quickly send it off (throw it) so you can get ready to catch the next. Then you do it all over again lest this ball hurtle to the ground and certain disaster.

Is that an accurate picture of what your life feels like? Can you relate to the picture of the juggler? If so, read on.

While there were some pain and struggles over the next several years, that tattered womb of Linda's conceived a second, a third, and then a fourth time. Elizabeth is now nineteen and in her sophomore year at Western Baptist College in Salem. She is a fine Christian young woman and is doing well as she prepares to become an elementary school teacher.

Following her is our first son, Josiah. How excited I was to have a son to play and wrestle and just do boy things with. He is intelligent and quick witted. Now sixteen, he loves playing soccer, spends way too much time on his computer, just received his drivers license, and I expect will make a profession somehow in the field of computers.

Following him was another son, Nathan, who is now fourteen. He has boundless energy and excitement and an overwhelming joy and passion for life. To me he seems to have the qualities, personality, and character to be a preacher someday. Coming home from a weeklong Christ in Youth conference recently he confirmed that yes, he felt the call of God to full-time ministry.

Finally is a third son, Micah, who is now twelve. Micah has affirmed for several years that when he grows up, he wants to be a missionary to

Kenya. He has the determination that this might just be the case. As Psalm 127:3, 5 says, "[Children] are a heritage from the LORD, . . . Blessed is the man whose quiver is full of them." My quiver was filling up, and God's blessings were flowing mightily into my life. Isn't it amazing the things God Almighty can do when we put our trust in him and let him work in our lives? The third great change of my life after moving to California—our family—was now well underway.

Returning to that juggling picture for a second, I could now throw away the tennis ball representing family and, with four kids, replace it with a softball. Juggling odd sized balls of growing demands was definitely becoming more challenging.

Intel

While Linda and school were well underway, my career at Intel was going better than I could have imagined.

In my job as a Quality and Assurance (Q+A) technician I had an opportunity to do a little programming work. I was interested in anything to do with computers and jumped at the chance. My boss began teaching me how to program in the C programming language. He would give me a few modest work assignments to move me along in my programming skills. Between my boss's tutelage, taking programming classes at college and my own self learning I was quickly acquiring this new skill. I also started to run the computer system of the Q+A department, which used the UNIX operating system.

I soon grew troubled by what seemed like an after the fact approach to quality and reliability at Intel. My thought was that rather than trying to test for quality after the chips were designed, maybe we could design reliability and test capabilities into the chips up front. Based on this notion, I started to teach myself about design and building test capabilities and self-testing circuitry directly into the chip. This sounded logical, and I began to engage with the chip design teams of the 80286. My hope was that I might get some of these ideas included in the 80386 design, which—with the 80286 coming to an end—was just about to get underway.

Intel had invented the microprocessor with the 4004 design in 1974. Others such as Motorola and National were jumping into this exciting new product area with designs of their own, though Intel remained the industry leader. Sometimes good, sometimes luck—Intel had won the all important IBM PC with our 8088/6 chip. The IBM PC was quickly proving to be "the design" that would redefine the entire industry. While the IBM PC was coming to the market later than other designs, it was not only a good design but also "open." The internal specifications were made available to others for their own innovation and enhancement. This became a watershed event for the world of computing, and the design quickly ushered in the personal computer as we know and love it today.

IBM had relied on two critical pieces of external technology to bring the PC to market, the microprocessor from Intel and the DOS operating system from Microsoft. Intel began to realize the strategic importance of this design win and the company was beginning to align itself behind this strategic position. As a result, the best and the brightest in the company were part of the microprocessor design team.

Picture this now-20-year-old kid, who knew nothing about chip design, halfway through his bachelor's degree in electrical engineering, approaching the "design team for the Intel microprocessor." (This needs to be read in reverent and hushed terms.) While not quite holy ground, that team was probably as close as you could get at that time in the industry.

Recall, I was passionate about computers, and one of the attractions of Intel was this crazy invention, the microprocessor. Up to this point I had been studying microprocessors or as a technician was doing some after the fact testing of them. This may sound just a touch sacrilegious, but I really felt that going to the "design team" was sort of like what Moses felt when approaching the burning bush. Wow, these were the real geniuses of the company. They really invent things. I thought they didn't walk; they just floated across the building and up and down the staircases. They worked on the most important projects for the company—as it turned out in retrospect, the most important projects for the entire industry. Everything they did was recorded in the journals of the industry. The products they created were changing the computer industry and the world. Well, while I was somewhat intimidated, I didn't hesitate to approach the design team with some of these crazy designs for quality and built-in self-test ideas.

Naturally, the design team said "of course, we'll immediately implement your ideas, it's a shame we didn't think of them ourselves."

Yeah, right. However, they saw this young, aggressive kid, working hard toward his bachelor degree, with some ideas that might be worth considering. Best of all, he knew UNIX. This latter point, UNIX, turned out to be my ticket into the chip design group. The 80386 team found these skills uniquely interesting and wanted me on the team. The designers were rebelling against the corporate IT group and planning on moving off the corporate IBM CMS environment to a UNIX based operating environment for their work. This UNIX environment promised to be more flexible and productive. Thus, while the Q+A department sent me to the design group to get the design for test capabilities built into the chip; the design team saw me as a chance to accelerate their rebellion to a UNIX environment. The design team quickly sucked me in, and I was never to return to Q+A.

After joining the design team, I cut my teeth on some wrap-up work for the 80286 design. Then, voila, I was engineer number four on the (drum roll, please) 80386 design team. I seriously thought this was as close to heaven as you could get for a professional role. I was thrilled to be part of microprocessor development for Intel. I could have never dreamed of a position this exciting when I started working for Intel. Life was good, and I was feeling very blessed.

I was learning how to design chips by day at Santa Clara and then later at Stanford. By night I was actually designing the most important chips in the industry.

One particular project at Stanford was sort of fun. If you've ever tried to use the shared mainframe computers on campus at the end of the quarter or semester, you realize that every other student is trying to do the same thing. The systems would go from their normal slow to hideously slow. Getting a terminal for computer time and getting a simulation done was next to impossible. Of course, I had more computers at my disposal at Intel than the entire campus had at Stanford. Not only that, but late at night, the normal time for students to really get to work, many of the mainframes at Intel were lightly loaded and I pretty much had them all to myself. Thus, on a certain class design project, while the rest of the class was struggling to get even one simulation done, I ran over 1,000 simulations of my design, literally perfecting it the night before the project was due.

Needless to say, I aced the class with sheer brute force on my side. While working and going to school was usually an extremely heavy load, on this one occasion, I was the only student on campus who got a decent night's sleep.

On another occasion, one of the well known professors on campus and in the industry described a new technique to design a binary 32 bit "adder" in class one day. An adder is one of the fundamental parts of the chip, used to add two numbers together. Typically it is used in numerous locations throughout a microprocessor design. Anything that could make this fundamental circuit run better would be hugely beneficial to the overall project. Well, as luck would have it—or another one of God's divine coincidence—I was designing the adder on the 80386 just then. Boy, was I excited. I immediately took his idea and thought that if it worked, I'd not only get this portion of the chip done quickly, but I'd look good to the whole design team as well.

After working on it for the next two days, I could prove that the idea didn't work. The adder that resulted wasn't any better than traditional approaches and in fact, was generally poorer in requiring even more chip area and consuming more power. With a bit of arrogant confidence, I went to this professor with reams of data and simulations under my arms to prove my point. The next two class periods became a public debate over the merits of his design.

I quickly moved through the design ranks, taking on increasing responsibilities in the chip project. A year after joining the 80386 design team, I began managing a couple of technicians who were doing schematics design. I had wanted to be the engineer, telling the technician what do, and I was excited about this new challenge. I completed one block of the chip, the instruction decoding unit, well ahead of schedule. I was then given a second unit to design, the main data path. Completing this, I moved on to tackling even a third, the protection and test logic. I eventually was put in charge of the final assembly and "tapeout."

If you could compare tapeout to an airplane design, it's like the final assembly of the very first airplane. The wings, engines, fuselage, landing gear and control systems are all independently designed by different sub-teams, and now we need to integrate them all in a finished product. Tapeout is the equivalent for chips, bringing all the units together into a complete design for the first time.

After the tapeout is complete, the design is sent to the enormous and expensive silicon fabrication facilities. After three to four weeks, the first silicon wafers come back to the design team for "debug." Debug is sort of like starting up the engines of the plane, testing to see if the flight control system really works, and checking whether the flaps and rudders operate correctly. Then comes the first test flight; can this thing really fly? If it has some problems, what are they? Where are the bugs and problems that our simulations didn't identify? Where did we make errors in the integration of the pieces into the whole? What changes are needed to get the chip working properly and ready to ramp into production?

The tapeout and debug process is extraordinarily visible to the company. After four years of laborious effort, mostly executed in relative solitude, now the world wants to know. The entire design team, the entire company, and hundreds of people at customers like IBM and Compaq are all anxious for updates and status, just like expectant parents and grandparents. Everyone has the same question—does it work? Needless to say, for someone of my age and level of experience, this was a huge level of responsibility.

This period was incredibly busy, intense and exhilarating. While the first chips "worked," they had some problems. We would quickly identify fixes to address those problems so we could continue to explore the chip and run more tests and software at it. We'd then identify more problems, for which we'd quickly work to identify additional fixes. This cycle continued in rapid succession for several months. Following this period of just getting it to work, we gradually shifted to focus on making it manufacturable. Why were some chips good and others failing? What were the marginalities in the design, and how could we fix each of these as well?

As we completed the tapeout and debug phases of the 80386 and it moved toward full production, I was pulled off to start the 80486 design as the original architect. Wow, employee number one on the next generation of the most important family of microprocessors on the planet. I labored on this for a year as well as some other tasks in development methodologies and some cleanup work on the 80386. About this time I completed my bachelors at Santa Clara and began working on my masters at Stanford. I had decided that working and going to school at the Ph.D. level wasn't a good idea. Due to residence requirements and the magnitude of the time commitments to complete a Ph.D., I wanted to take it easy and not be doing full time work and school. After applying to a number of schools, I was accepted and received a full scholarship to the University of Illinois at Urbana Champaign. Intel unexpectedly received my resignation as I was ready to move to the next phase of studies.

On this and two other occasions, I resigned from Intel to finish my Ph.D. However, I found it hard to leave. Instead of seeing me to the door, they kept finding creative ways to keep me challenged and committed to the company. I recall a conversation with the president of Intel at the time, the legendary Andy Grove, who said, "Do you want to go to school and learn to fly on the simulator, or do you want to stay here and fly the real jet?"

To challenge me to stay at this point, I was offered the position of 80486 design manager. Imagine this, the crown jewels of Intel, the most important chip project in the industry, and I—barely out of college, having just finished my masters, a whopping twenty-five years old, much less experienced than many of the people who would be working for me—was being offered the chance to run the whole project. I was flattered but also somewhat overwhelmed with the magnitude of the challenge and responsibilities. Oh yes, in case you hadn't guessed by now, I decided to stay on board at Intel and "fly the jet." If being a designer on the 80386 was close to heaven, being the design manager of the 80486 was like the second heaven. I was enjoying myself beyond measure.

Following the 80386 and 80486 projects and over the ensuing years, my career has continued to progress rapidly. For fifteen years, I received a promotion every year. I moved through being the design manager of the 80486, the 486DX2 and the Pentium Pro. All these chips carried the company and the industry for their period of significance and leadership. I became the general manager of our video conferencing and communications product, initiating many of the key technologies that have made the Internet a broad replacement for traditional switched voice telephony.

I was given the honor of being promoted to VP at the age of thirty-two, the youngest in the history of the company. I got the mammoth assignment of being the General Manager of desktop products, the largest business unit of the company, representing tens of billions in revenue. At thirty-five I became a corporate officer and joined the executive staff, the highest management body at Intel. I was then made a corporate VP and group Chief Technology Officer for the primary business of the company.

In the fall of 2001 I was promoted to be the first ever Chief Technology Officer for Intel Corporation at the ripe old age of forty. Imagine the honor of being the CTO for one of the most technologically significant companies of the last fifty years. Imagine being the CTO of a company that had people like Gordon Moore, Andy Grove and Robert Noyce, legends in the industry, as the primary technical drivers for many years. I've been so blessed that it's simply overwhelming.

Of course, while God's hand has been mighty upon me, I also have to pause and give great recognition to my employer, Intel. How many places are truly merit based in their decisions on promotions and assignments? How many employers would take the risk of putting a twenty-five year old kid in charge of the crown jewels of the corporation's future? Over and over, Intel has given me opportunities, challenges, and rewards of tremendous degree.

At this point, let's return to the imagery of the juggler. One tennis-sized ball was for work, another was for God, and we had already graduated to a softball-sized ball for family. Well, throw away the tennis ball for work; it was now the size of a soccer ball.

Church

Though family, school, and work take most of my time, Linda and I have always remained active in our local congregation. We began a Bible study in our home and, except for the year we moved from California to Oregon, we have continued this practice. We've now had a study in our home for over seventeen years. We've found this to be a great blessing, an opportunity to share our faith with others and build many long term relationships. As our children go out on their own, I can only hope they will recall this example and find or host study and fellowship groups of their own.

Linda has volunteered at both school and church. At one point we thought we'd like to teach a Sunday school class together. However, she has ended up loving her two- and three-year-olds, and I'm an adult teacher periodically throughout the year. Every time we tried to compromise at something like junior high . . . well . . . it was a disaster.

You'll see a bit later in my personal mission statement that I put down as a goal to "become an elder in my local congregation." When I wrote that I expected I would fulfill that when I was old and wise . . . maybe age fifty. However, writing something like that can be a little dangerous. When our minister preached a sermon on what biblical eldership was all about and the need for men to take roles of leadership in their families and their church, I was pierced to the heart. While I remained silent, I knew well what was coming. I had written these goals years before and now felt God's moving in my heart. A few months later, I was called to be an elder. I'm currently serving my sixth year as an elder at Singing Hills Christian Church in Hillsboro, Oregon.

Summary

If you hadn't guessed yet, I'm a busy guy, and I enjoy being busy. It gets my adrenaline going. When I die, I want to be used up for God, having given everything I can to do my best for his kingdom. I never want to retire. In fact, I would challenge any to show where God suggests that people should retire. Passages like Philippians 3:14, 1 Corinthians 9:24-26 and Galatians 2:2 create a picture of a marathon runner going the whole distance and running hard to the finish line—graduation to the heavenly kingdom at the end of one's life on earth. So I simply want to move from one type of job to another as God leads. At some point along the way, I may stop working at a secular position, but it won't be for lack of ministry and work that I'm entirely involved in and consumed by.

In personality style, I'm a "driver" or "Type A." I am zealous to achieve and overachieve. I work hard and am competitive and aggressive. I have tendencies to be a workaholic. I can tell tale upon tale of intense weeks. At the end of the 80386 project, the "tapeout team" was working twenty-hour days. Each of us would go home a bit, eat a bit, sleep a bit and come back six or seven hours later to work another twenty or so hours. If you do the math, you'll notice that's twenty-six- or twenty-seven-hour days. After a week or so of twenty-seven-hour days, you start to lose a day in there somewhere. One night I was so terribly exhausted that I just crawled under my desk to be wakened by voices the next morning . . . I was encouraged that they were real voices.

Maybe one particular frenetic week will give you some perspective on what my life can be like. Of course, some of you reading this might say "been there." Others might feel a bit of pride or competitive spirit and declare "I can top that!" If so, I have one more for you in chapter 4. If you can top that one as well, you win and I will make no attempt to keep you from claiming to be the world's busiest person:

• Sunday after church in the morning, left early for my flight to Taiwan.

• Of course, long flights are a great time to catch up, so I worked on E-mail and my computer almost the entire trip.

• Landed Monday night in Taiwan. Immediately went from the airport to the stage for a speech dry run.

• Tuesday morning I was the kickoff keynote speaker to a thousand or so.

• Immediately following the speech, I had a press conference, which was followed by back-to-back customer meetings all day.

• Tuesday night was a large Intel gathering; had to stay awake during the speeches, being a table host and other official duties. Hard to keep my head out of the hot and sour soup. . . .

• Wednesday morning additional customer meetings in Taipei.

• Left Taiwan Wednesday afternoon and flew to Hong Kong, arriving late.

• Thursday morning we crossed over into mainland China to Shen Zhen in the morning for customer meetings.

• Back to Hong Kong in the afternoon for customer meetings.

• Flew from Hong Kong to Beijing at night, arriving very late.

• Friday back-to-back day of customer meetings, press interviews and internal operations reviews.

• Late dinner in Beijing with management team at our office.

• While Saturday was supposed to be a free day, emergency situation arose with Korean customer.

• Flew from Beijing to Seoul, Korea, for negotiations in the afternoon.

• Flew back from Seoul to Beijing on Saturday night.

• Speech on Sunday to a packed audience at Beijing University.

• After speech, left Beijing to fly to Tokyo.

• Monday was packed with customer meetings, a fair-sized press conference, and an internal operations review, followed by a traditional Japanese customer dinner that lasted late into the evening.

• Tough negotiation on Tuesday morning, other customer meetings during the morning and off to Narita airport in the afternoon.

• Flew home all day on Tuesday, worked almost all the way on mail and computer.

• Arrived home in the morning in U.S. on Tuesday after crossing the International Date Line. After freshening up, immediately went into an all-day meeting at Intel.

• Flew Wednesday to New Orleans for a speech dry run that night.

• Speech to 2000 or so at Microsoft's WinHec conference on Thursday morning, flew home that night to Portland.

• Friday was frantic day trying to catch up at work from being gone from office for almost two weeks.

• Friday night . . . drove with the family up to Seattle.

• Gave Puget Sound Christian College commencement speech on Saturday morning.

• After attending a graduation party that afternoon, drove back to Portland.

• Sunday morning church, I gave the offering and communion meditations. Quiet afternoon with our family on Sunday.

• Monday, up at 4 A.M. , to catch the first flight to California.

• All day Monday in strategic planning session in California.

• Normal internal meetings all day Tuesday. Home late Tuesday night on last flight to Portland.

• Wednesday up at 5 A.M. , to work by 6:30, worked till 5 P.M.

• Led our home Bible study Wednesday night.

• Thursday, racquetball game at 6:30 A.M. , normal workday 8 to 5.

• Thursday night, working on juggling speech.

• Friday, first meeting at 7 A.M. , normal meetings all day.

• Friday night, flew to California for a men's conference.

• Saturday morning, gave juggling speech at Northern California Evangelistic Association Men's Advance.

• Flew home Saturday in the afternoon and, gasp, done, with this three-week march.

While that list may look unbelievable, yes, it was a real three week period which ranks near the top of my all time crazy weeks. Being in Asia for a workaholic is great. You get to work all day and into the evening on "Asia time." Then when you get back to your hotel, you don't go to sleep, you do email and phone calls and join meetings back in the U.S. Thus, you are typically working about double time every

day. I'd also point out, about halfway through this list, the three con-
secutive Tuesdays. For a workaholic, crossing the International Date
Line is exciting. You work a day in Asia, flying home you work a second day on the long 10+ hours of flying home, and finally you land in
the morning on the West Coast, giving you the opportunity to work
your third Tuesday after you arrive. I am somewhat comforted by Peter
Drucker's insight: "A leader is a mono-maniac on a mission." I qualify.

Before bringing this chapter to a close, I'd like to go back one last
time to that picture of a juggler. Softball for family, a soccer ball for
work, and a tennis ball for God. Well, by this time, the kids have hit
the teenage years, so throw the softball away for family. Those
teenagers are now a bit odd, and they are better represented by an odd
shaped football. So, start juggling:

- a tennis ball for God,
- a football for family,
- and a soccer ball for work.

Juggling is hard enough under the best of circumstances, but if you
throw in some odd shapes and larger items, it gets really hard. Can you
relate to this kind of experience and picture? If so, the following seven
chapters of proven and practical advice should help you to manage better.

Questions

At the end of each chapter I've included a set of questions. These
are meant for personal use as you ponder your life and apply the chapter material. These could also be used in a class setting as discussion
topics; I've used them this way myself. Most of the questions are taken
from those I've received as I've presented this material over the years.
While they are included here simply in question form, in the appendix
I've also included each question with the answer that I would give
from my personal life.

Many of these questions are personal and have no right or wrong
answer. They're meant as much to provoke thought, discussion, and
action as to have you provide answers. I'd encourage you to answer
them and share your thoughts with your spouse, close friend, and/or
mentors, then begin to work on your priorities for your own life.

Chapter 1: Q&A

Note: my own responses to these questions can be found at the end of this book.

1. Many people would argue that the Internet is evil. What do you believe about it and other technologies that have been used in questionable manners?

2. The founder of Xerox, Chester Carlson, attributed his sustenance during difficult times to the 'Geeta,' the Hindu spiritual text. Don't you think that being spiritual is more important, whether you are a Christian, Hindu, or Muslim?

3. In your time with God, do you ask God for help with your work or profession? Does God provide ideas, witty inventions, or specific help in the workplace? Do you have some ways to know what way to proceed, what direction to take in your work?

4. How does the average person cope with commitments to God and family compared to others who are far more capable or talented? Don't average people need to work even harder to be great employees, making achieving balance impossible for the average person?

5. How do you know if you are in the right profession? Could the struggle with balance be because you are doing the wrong thing?

CHAPTER 2

Personal Mission Statement

Imagine that tomorrow morning, without warning, you loudly announce to the family, "We're going to leave today on vacation. Get ready to go right now!" Of course, having no forewarning, your kids and spouse are a bit startled and start asking dumb questions like:

"Where are we going?" to which you respond, "I don't know."

"What are we going to do?" to which you respond, "I haven't decided yet."

"How are we going to get there?" to which you respond, "Not sure, but we'll figure it out after we get started."

After a few bewildered looks, you demand, "Pack your things, we're leaving in fifteen minutes."

To which your kids, now even more perplexed, reply, "How can we pack? We don't know where we going."

"What should we take? We don't know what we're going to do."

"How many days are we going to be gone?"

To which you reply, "I'm not sure about any of that, but grab whatever you want for vacation and let's go. We're leaving in fourteen minutes!"

Of course, this is a silly scenario. You don't just up and leave on vacation without any planning. You always have at least some sort of plan in mind, even when you're trying to be flexible and spontaneous. Is it a driving vacation, or are you flying somewhere? Or maybe you are going camping or on a weeklong cruise. Are you going for just a day or two or a couple of weeks?

I have one good friend who almost lives for vacations. Every time I talk with him, he's telling me about this rafting trip, that hunting outing, or a ski trip he has planned for a year or even two or three in the future. His vacation plans consume the majority of his discretionary time.

All of us will spend significant time and energy planning for a vacation. We'll develop an itinerary, purchase tickets, and make reservations. Likewise with major purchases like a car or a home, or decisions like choosing a child's college, we'll do thorough research and enlist the help and advice of others, and sometimes even get professional assistance. At work, if given a big assignment by the boss, we'll plan every aspect of the job in detail.

So what's the point? While most of us will spend considerable energy planning in other areas, far too few of us have seriously considered and planned our most critical assets and most limited resource: our gifts and our time. Do you have a destination in mind for your life? Do you have a strategy for how you are going to get there? How will you know when you've hit a critical milestone or when you have fallen off course? What do you want to accomplish?

When I hit about thirty-one or thirty-two years of age, I began to sense some aimlessness and confusion. After moving to California in 1979 to start my career at Intel, I had in mind a set of goals I wanted to accomplish. I just hadn't developed them formally or written them down, but I had a pretty clear set of things in my mind I wanted to accomplish.

I had wanted to become an engineer, and I reached that goal with my promotion to engineer after joining the design team of the 80386 in 1982.

After getting married—and given Linda's medical condition—we had a goal to start a family. Linda desired two children; I was more aggressive and said eight. We took the geometric mean and settled on four.

I wanted to complete my education, and I got my bachelors from Santa Clara in 1983, finished my masters from Stanford in 1985, and decided against attempting to finish a Ph.D., at least for the time being.

I had always wanted to be an inventor. I received my first patent on April 12, 1988, for the "Optimally Partitioned Regenerative Carry Lookahead Adder."

After finishing school, and with at least some discretionary time freed up, I began writing a book with the architect of the 80386, John Crawford. Finishing a book became another goal, and Programming the 80386 was published by Sybex in 1987.

I wanted to move to a more family oriented location to raise our kids. Oregon fit the bill nicely, and in 1990 we relocated to Beaverton, Oregon.

I wanted to complete some significant projects at Intel, things I could forever look back at as my accomplishments. Having played a significant role in developing two of the most important chip projects in the industry, that goal was completed as well.

I also wanted to increase my role and relevance at Intel, and I became the youngest VP in the history of the company at thirty-two years old.

All of a sudden, I found myself struggling with the question of what I wanted to do with the rest of my life. What else did I want to accomplish? I felt as if the rudder had been taken off my ship.

Through some reading, I stumbled onto the idea of writing a personal mission statement. Now, that might sound easy, but for me and most everyone I've talked to it's quite difficult. It requires arduous self-reflection and prayer. I struggled to finish mine for over a year. I wrote drafts and then threw them away. Wrote them again and filed them away. Pulled them out a few months later and revised them, over and over.

You might ask, how does this process square with the familiar instruction found in James 4:13-15? Here's what the passage says:

> Now listen, you who say, "Today or tomorrow we will go to this or that city, spend a year there, carry on business and make money." Why, you do not even know what will happen tomorrow. What is your life? You are a mist that appears for a little while and then vanishes. Instead, you ought to say, "If it is the Lord's will, we will live and do this or that."

While on the surface there seems to be conflict, I don't think there really is. Let me explain. God has placed into each of us a set of gifts and skills. Psalm 139:14 says each of us is "wonderfully made" or, in the King James Version, "curiously wrought." Romans 12:6 tells us, "We have different gifts, according to the grace given us. If a man's gift is prophesying, let him use it in proportion to his faith."

God takes the unique creation of each individual and then extols the virtues of using our talents to do great things for the kingdom:

> "Well done, my good servant!" his master replied. "Because you have been trustworthy in a very small matter, take charge of ten cities." (Luke 19:17)

He even chastises those who choose to leave their talents unused:

Then he said to those standing by, "Take his mina away from him and give it to the one who has ten minas." (Luke 19:24)

He praises those who create fruit for the kingdom:

This is to my Father's glory, that you bear much fruit, showing yourselves to be my disciples. (John 15:8)

He encourages his followers to develop themselves and to seek leadership in the church. He praises the craftsman, he considers learning and knowledge a gift to be carefully utilized, and he extols the woman of Proverbs 31 for her wisdom and planning. Thus, we find plenty of support for the idea of developing a Personal Mission Statement in the Scriptures.

What do we make, then, of James 4? Instead of dissuading us from planning our lives, I believe the passage addresses people who ignore the certain eventual return of our Lord Jesus Christ—who try to live as if God doesn't exist and they're not responsible to him.

So, I offer up below an excerpted version of my personal mission statement as an example you might find helpful in crafting your own. I'd like to make clear that this is my mission statement, values, and goals. I'm still far from accomplishing several of the items listed. This isn't a statement of what I've done, but of what I aspire to become. This isn't a picture of who I am but of what I believe God has created me to become. I continue to strive for them, and working toward them is exactly the purpose in writing them down.

Of course, any such work is a very personal affair. My gifts and passions from God are different from yours. My bent is not your bent. Consider these nothing more than a template that might be somewhat helpful in crafting your own.

I would also challenge you that you must, as I had to, go through your period of soul searching in developing your personal mission statement. This is hard work, and it's foolish to think you'll be able to knock them out in a few hours on a weekend. You may get something down on a piece of paper that quickly, but those goals won't pass the test of time. This is a deep, soul searching exercise; plan on dwelling on them for a while, and when you're finished you'll have something useful for many years to come. After I completed mine, I've only made one round of minor modifications to them over the last eight years and a small bit of wordsmithing while writing this book.

A few other comments as you consider drafting your own: After you have a draft you like, ask your spouse to read it. Ask if this is the kind of person he or she hopes you will become. While I firmly believe these are personal goals, you need to know if where you want to go with your life and where your spouse wants you to go are reasonably well aligned. If you find they are not, this exercise may be a great way to identify some long term areas of conflict with your spouse that you haven't recognized before. If they are aligned, this is a good opportunity to gain your mate's support and encouragement for this lifelong, purpose-filled mission you are now committing yourself toward.

I'd also suggest you have a small number of trusted friends or mentors (more on this in chapter 6) read them as well. Ask if these goals are consistent with your character and personality. Their independent perspective on you is probably more valuable than you can fathom.

My Personal Mission Statement

Mission: I will be a Christian Husband, Family Man, and Businessman. I will use every resource God provides me to carry out His work on earth as set forth below.

Values: The things I will stand for, my values I will be recognized for. I will:

1. Work hard in all that I do. (Col. 3:23)

2. Give my best effort in every task. (1 Thes. 4:1)

3. Be open to the direction of the Holy Spirit wherever that may lead. (John 14:26)

4. Enthusiastically approach new challenges and all else I do. (2 Cor. 9:2)

5. Live by Christian principles. In all things I will try to make Christ's ethics and morals my own. (Rom. 2:7-8)

6. Be open, honest, and generous. (2 Cor. 9:11)

7. Be careful with words and actions. (James 1:26)

8. Seek the counsel of others frequently and thoughtfully. (Prov. 15:22)

9. Never be satisfied with the status quo. I will be an agent of change. (Rom. 15:20)

10. Seek to improve and grow those around and beneath me in work and all other areas. (1 Thes. 5:14)

11. Not seek my own glory, I will seek to honor God and have praise be given to those around me. (Rom. 15:5-6)

12. Never take things too seriously but have a great time in everything, continually enjoying God's blessings. (James 4:13-15)

Goals: The things I will accomplish, my goals. I will:

1. Make my marriage an example of that laid out in the Scriptures. I will be a one-woman man seeking the growth of my wife. I will assist her in the duties of our household, date her regularly, and cherish her always.

2. Have all four of my children make personal commitments of faith to Christ, publicly demonstrating their new life through baptism. Play an active role in leading them into Christian maturity.

3. Assist in bringing to Christ or to a much greater degree of Christian maturity over 100 people.

4. Write a book explaining the things God has taught me through life for my children, grandchildren, and great grandchildren.

5. Generate substantial wealth for my employer.

6. Become president of Intel Corporation. I will do so while maintaining my values and ethics.

7. Be an elder of the congregation at which we worship.

8. Give an increasing portion of all I earn to charity: church, missions, and other Christian organizations.

9. Provide financially for my wife, children, and grandchildren.

10. Spend quality and quantity time with my children while they are young. On average, I will dedicate ten hours per week to personal time with them.

11. Visit over fifty foreign countries to develop a broad world view and a passion for all of God's children.

12. Assist others who are Christians to achieve success in their profession and careers.

13. Continually be in the Word of God. I will be in the Word on a daily basis. I will read the Bible through at least twice each year.

14. Memorize Scripture. I will add to my repertoire at least ten new verses each year.

15. Continue to read—I will read at least five significant books each year.

16. Continue to learn—I will pick up at least one new topic, sport, field, or craft per year.

17. Continue to teach—I will teach at least one class each year.

18. Become fluent in at least one additional language.

19. I will fast one day per week for the spiritual health and protection of my children.

20. Exercise regularly, at least three times per week.

21. Lead weekly Bible Study.

I found that developing the three sections worked very well. If you've read other works on this subject, they may or may not follow this type of structure. Use any format you like and on any material you like, paper plates or napkins included. However, the three sections have some utility:

Mission: A simple short statement. If you were going to have your epitaph written tomorrow, what would you want it to say? If you can answer that, that's a good place to start. If not, it's time to start some serious self-examination. In my Mission statement the two key words are "every resource." When my time on earth is complete I want to be like Paul and have run the good race (2 Tim. 4:7) and used up every ounce of energy, minute of time, and dollar of resources for his purpose and kingdom.

Values: For me, these are the statements I want people to make immediately when asked "What's Pat like?" Recently I was challenged on some behaviors I've exhibited at Intel over the years and was pointedly asked if I thought people would consider them consistent with my Christian faith. I was prone to overstate my accomplishments while sometimes demeaning the work of others. I also would want to own and control topics and resources for which I should rather have been more appropriately a mere stakeholder or even a consultant. Sadly, I had to confess that no, those behaviors were not consistent with my faith and the person I desire to become. I was cut to the heart, and I was prompted to strong corrective action.

Goals: Get specific enough that you can regularly measure your progress against these goals. Hopefully over many years you will accomplish some of these and be able to check them off as completed. Several might be continual, such as read so many books per year or exercise so many times per week. Others will come and go as you reach certain milestones, such as baptizing your last child into a personal relationship with Christ or writing a book. A couple of comments on some of my goals:

> # 4. Write a book explaining the things God has taught me through life for my children, grandchildren, and great grandchildren.

As I was encouraged to consider writing this book by several who had heard my juggling talk, I came face to face with my personal mission statement. Without this written down as a clear goal, I don't think I'd have undertaken the work you are now reading. Also, as I wrote this goal many years ago, I wanted to pass on what I've learned to future generations of my offspring. As such, I've tried to make this a much more personal work than I would have otherwise. I also expect that I'll need to revise the book in future years as God continues to train me.

> # 7. Be an elder of the congregation at which we worship.

As noted above, given this was already on my mission statement, I couldn't ignore the request when I was asked to serve in this capacity. Without having written this some years earlier, I would have probably rationalized away the request, saying "some time in the future." As we know, the future never really gets here. Instead, we need to set goals and priorities and then live by them.

9. Provide financially for my wife, children, and grand-children.

This led us to develop wills and trusts for Linda, our children, and myself about seven years ago. Recently we entirely revised them, reflecting more of our current financial situation as well as looking forward to future generations. If you haven't yet written them, I'd challenge you to do so soon. In many states and countries, the lack of financial plans and wills may lead to substantial additional taxes, as well as to a much greater public disclosure of your financial status (or lack thereof). Proper financial planning, trusts, and wills can assure confidentiality is maintained while the maximum transfer of financial worth occurs to your family and charities as you and your spouse desire.

Your goals might be radically different from mine. They might include: Buying a home, getting out of debt, going into the ministry, starting your own business, finding a Christian spouse, choosing and completing a degree, starting a new church, going on short or long term missions, adopting a child, specific financial goals, family goals etc. Let your mind wander some, brainstorm more, and when you're done, your mission statement should be something that makes your passions swell.

After your statement is finished, come back and just read it every couple of months. Ask yourself if you've been making progress toward those values and goals. On most occasions when I read mine, I see an area I should be doing more, or I'll reflect on some actions or incidents where I failed to execute according to my values. I'll often decide on some additional actions I need to take toward a particular goal.

Generally, I find these readings uplifting as I'll see at least some areas of progress, and the passion of what I'm to become always encourages me forward. Sometimes, they can be depressing as well. Looking at a picture of what you want to become and seeing your inadequacies can be discouraging; particularly after a bad week or month or two. I'd also suggest you occasionally stick a copy under your spouse's nose (or that of a close friend) and ask, is this still the person you want me to become?

Once a year, grade your progress toward your goals. I keep a spreadsheet in which I specifically grade each year how I did against each of the twenty-one goals noted above. How many books did I read, and what were the titles and authors? Did I meet my Scripture reading and memory goals? (For many years this was an area I wasn't consistently developing, though my goals had stated I would.) I pull out the tax forms and calculate how well we did against our giving goals, and then I plan the appropriate giving objectives and specific giving plan for next year. I tend to do this "grading" at tax time, April 15. I'm already depressed with taxes so I need not worry about the bad grading I may have to give myself. Also, it's a good time since all the financial data are handy and fresh in my mind as well.

Praise the Lord, some of my goals are mostly completed, as is the case with number two. All four of my children have now accepted Christ as their Lord and Savior. Even though this goal is partially complete, I enjoy reflecting positively on it, and thus I don't bother to revise the overall list. Also, since the second half of this goal states "lead them into Christian maturity," it challenges me to continue to pray for them. It also inspires me to find ways to encourage them to remain strong in the faith and continue to live in a manner reflecting their decision to follow Christ.

At this point I would exhort you to DO IT. I recently had lunch with a good friend who wanted to work on his priorities. Knowing of my teaching and book-writing on this subject, he had asked for a copy of this manuscript. Our lunch meeting was several months later, and he had commented on several occasions in the interim how much he appreciated the manuscript and how helpful it was as he began his own journey of becoming a better juggler.

After we had discussed different items for a while, I asked him pointedly if in fact he had written down his personal mission statement. He sheepishly replied he hadn't. I was a bit taken aback. He needed to start writing. I was discouraged that he wanted to "get together and talk" having not even taken seriously his need to do some soul searching and work. I made it clear that before we would meet again, I expected him to have completed a substantive draft of his own mission statement.

Likewise, I pray that you will use my personal mission statement to help you in developing your own, and that the exercise will give you a stronger sense of purpose and direction for your life. You do not want to be living randomly from day to day, but with purpose for the rest of your life. A focused life has great power.

Discipline

No discussion of priorities could be complete without some discussion of personal discipline.

As Linda and I were dating, on more than one occasion she expressed disappointment with the amount of time I spent with her. She saw her friends getting a much bigger share of their boyfriend's time than she had of mine. In response, as mentioned earlier, I developed a detailed assessment of the time I spent on each activity during the week. I laid out on a 24-hour-day, 7-days-a-week chart all the time that was to be dedicated to school, to studying, to work, to church, to chores, to sleep, to her, and to personal leisure; and after all of that, I indicated whatever was left over.

Then I reviewed the chart in detail with Linda. Her response was, "you don't have any more hours." In fact, I didn't; my schedule was completely full. I clearly understood where the hours were going, and they were aligned with my priorities at the time. While it was difficult, Linda better understood and could accept the data.

I recommend you do a similar planning exercise. Make an estimate of how many hours each week you take for the major activities of your life: work, school, rest, hobbies, spouse, children, commuting, church and God, etc. Then, over a typical period of your life, take two weeks and do a detailed time study. Keep track of how you spend your time, using 15- to 30-minute increments. After you have gathered the raw data, categorize them carefully. Finally, with the summary in hand, make the difficult assessments. Ask yourself:

- Any surprises? Areas where I just couldn't imagine I was wasting—er, uh, um, spending—so much of my time?
- Is this where I want my time to go?
- Am I putting as much time as I'd like into the areas I want as the priorities in my life?
- How much time am I really spending with my spouse? Children? Friends?
- Did I realize how much time I was spending at work?

As you finish your personal mission statement, you'll probably end up with more goals than you have time to pursue. Where will those extra hours come from? A detailed time study can reveal hidden diamonds in your day. Do you really need to sleep that long or are you being just a bit lazy? If you wanted to, could you crawl out of bed a bit earlier on weekends and get in more physical exercise or time with your children? Is playing three rounds of golf each week really that important to you? Could some of those hours in front of the television be spent instead truly focused on your mate?

In no way am I condemning any of those activities. Maybe building relationships on the golf course is absolutely consistent with your mission statement. It may be the foundation for your career or the time when you can mentor others (more on that subject in chapter 6). Maybe you do want to spend a good amount of your leisure time watching sports—great! I'm only challenging you to make these conscious decisions based on thoughtful consideration and planning.

With my chaotic lifestyle and all the travel I do, including many meals in fine restaurants, I've found it hard to exercise and easy to put on unwanted pounds and inches. Thus, I set a goal of getting back to my marriage weight. I began getting into the habit of packing my running shoes and shorts for overnight trips (and booking into hotels with good workout facilities), and arranged a friendly competition with Linda. Using a few spare minutes here and there, I've gotten myself into better shape than I'd enjoyed for the past fifteen years.

Don't finish all your corrective action plans just yet, though. Wait until you've finished a couple more chapters. I have a few more tools and priorities for you to consider before you compile your "action required" list.

Finally, I'd encourage you to periodically redo your time study. The first time I did this for myself, I was in school and my time was well structured and accounted for. While some of the categorized data were a bit startling, I was pretty much living by my priorities in that season of my life.

The second time I did the time study, the findings were more surprising. I was out of school, and my schedule had become more dynamic and much less structured. Thus, the results of this study had a much greater impact.

What I discovered was that finishing work on my master's degree meant more time available for Intel. Managing the 80486 project, with more than 100 people now reporting to me, gave me a huge sense of responsibility. Every mistake or problem became my personal mission. As the flight director said in the movie *Apollo 13*, "Failure is not an option." And the surest way to prevent it was to work more hours.

The time study revealed I was routinely putting in more than eighty hours per week. My "get home" time kept getting later and later. Seeing those results in black and white shouldn't have been a surprise—Linda had been sending all the signals I should have needed for months—but it was.

Over the years, each succeeding study has brought fewer surprises, but I've still been challenged to make changes to my activities every single time.

This probably sounds like a lot of work, and frankly, it is. However, let's remember that our time is our most precious resource. We can't stop or even slow its passage, and we can't get more of it. Our time on earth is like a vapor that disappears quickly (James 4:14). But we can make conscious and specific decisions on how we use it. So, while getting a handle on it can be laborious, the alternative is to naively lose track of this priceless resource. (See chapter 6 for how a mentor can help you keep your use of time in line with your priorities.)

Chapter 2 Q&A

1. Why do you really need to prepare a Personal Mission Statement with specific values and goals?

2. What kind of time management tools do you use?

3. How does one set goals or mission statements when the world around us changes so fast?

4. How should one go about developing a will and detailed financial plan for his or her family?

CHAPTER 3

Prioritize God

One particularly challenging week at Intel, I had a number of customer meetings to attend and several presentations to give. I felt especially anxious about a CSD (corporate strategic discussion) presentation I was to be making. The topic was highly contentious, it represented a substantial business risk for the company, and all the top management would be there, including Gordon Moore and Andy Grove.

The only way to prepare to lead such a discussion is to put in a lot of time and effort. That meant several late-night working sessions for the team and I, and all this in addition to my normally heavy workload.

One result was that my personal devotional times went out the window that week. No feeding of my spirit, no laying of my burdens before the Lord in prayer. By the time the big presentation rolled around, I was exhausted, nervous, and way out of spiritual balance.

Not surprisingly, though the team and some coaching from peers got me through, the strategy we proposed was considered weak and was challenged by Andy in particular. I felt tired and inadequate in carrying out the rest of my duties as well. By the end of the week I was kicking myself, knowing I'd had to relearn a lesson I never should have forgotten—make time daily for God. I've heard it said that maturity is learning the lessons you thought you already knew.

I could put no single item more firmly in this category than the need to prioritize daily time with God. How often I've gotten myself mired in a long and dreadful day, struggling with issue after issue, feeling nothing could go right and seeing nothing but darker and more ominous clouds on the horizon. Somewhere in that ugly, hurried and hazy fog of daily activities, I'll be pricked back to a spiritual consciousness and ask myself, have you been in God's Word today? Have you had your daily devotions and prayer time? Have you left these issues and concerns at the throne of the Father?

Time and again, the answer will be no, I haven't been in the Word or in prayer. Yet again, I had decided that God isn't really capable of carrying or helping with these burdens. I can better handle them all by myself. Once again, as in that dreadful week at Intel, Paul's cries seem so appropriate.

> I do not understand what I do. For what I want to do I do not do, but what I hate I do. And if I do what I do not want to do, I agree that the law is good. As it is, it is no longer I myself who do it, but it is sin living in me. I know that nothing good lives in me, that is, in my sinful nature. For I have the desire to do what is good, but I cannot carry it out. (Romans 7:15-18)

How refreshing to come to the throne of the Father and be united with him in prayer and study of his Word. I've not sat down and kept statistics for good vs. bad days, but I can assert with confidence that I handle the rough days so much better if I've been in the Word and prepared myself for the day with my God and Father. How different a countenance I carry now. My attitude is better, my patience more robust, my tongue more careful, my discernment greater, and my patience increased (especially when I realize my real employer is not Intel but my heavenly Lord and Father).

As I've had to struggle with this challenge over the years, I've tried to develop some little habits that help to bring to mind my daily devotion time.

During the period I was going to school and into the early part of my Intel career, if something wasn't technology related or directly applicable to school or work, I didn't bother with it. In fact, on one occasion I was so focused that the world was "blowing up" and I wasn't even aware.

After Mount Saint Helens erupted on Tuesday, May 18, 1980, Linda and I were together for our regular Friday night date. She mentioned something about the eruption, and I asked what she was talking about. It had been the largest volcanic eruption in recent memory. The Northwest looked like a war zone, skies over much of the nation were clouded with volcanic ash, millions of acres of lush forest had evaporated in just a few minutes, and I didn't even know about it three days later.

Early in my time at Intel, however, Andy Grove challenged me to read daily *The Wall Street Journal*. I made it a habit, and over the fifteen years since then, I've read it more than 90 percent of the time. I started to see, though, that on occasion I would get in my *Journal* without getting in my Bible. From this, I committed to never read the *Journal* prior to finishing my daily devotional time. This has created a natural reminder for me. Daily as I reach for the *Journal*, I'm again prompted to go to God's Word.

I wish I could report a perfect success record since I put this regimen into place. But sometimes I oversleep, other times I get too easily preoccupied with something I'm working on, and other times, it turns out to be just a difficult week.

While each of us is different, I'd encourage you to find that habit or event that will encourage you to make time for personal devotions every day. Maybe you make a commitment to God that his Word and prayer come before coffee and donuts. Maybe you'll decide to talk to God before you make your first phone call of the day. Or perhaps your thought will be that you feed your spirit before feeding your body, or that you nourish your soul before exercising your physique. If you're a night person, you might choose to lay your life before the Father before letting your body rest.

This latter one doesn't work for me. Trying to have devotions in bed after a long day is generally sure to put me to sleep. Whatever works for you—however you need to bribe yourself, encourage yourself, abuse yourself, or reward yourself—do it. Find something that will prick your consciousness and remind your brain so that daily devotions become a habit.

When I travel, I generally have my prayer time on the way to the airport. It's usually early in the morning and about a forty-minute drive. After grabbing my morning latte at my favorite coffee stand, I'll sing a few hymns or praise songs to start out with. I then pray through the "ACTS" acronym as I'm making the drive to the airport on the other side of town:

A. acknowledgment—Praising God for who he is, what he is, and what marvelous things he has done. Specifically bringing to mind areas and ways I've seen him at work, and acknowledging him as the God, Father, Creator, and Savior.

C.   Confession—specifically laying before the throne my sins, yet again calling on the body and blood of the Savior to cleanse me from all unrighteousness. Praying for future strength and wisdom to combat these areas of sin in my life.

T.   Thanksgiving—Thanking him for the numerous blessings he has given me. Specifically calling to mind family members and events of the day or week for which I am particularly thankful.

S.   Supplication—Making those specific requests that I have for the Father. I always pray for the daily needs of my wife and each of the children by name. I pray that each of the kids might be holy and pure before God; that they might be useful in their professions for him; that their future spouses are being set aside in holiness and purity for them; and that their future in-laws are holding their children up in prayer as I am mine. By the time our kids have married, thousands of prayers will have gone up to the Father for them and their future spouses. I also pray for my church, minister, missionaries and fellow elders, and, finally, the requests of my shepherding group, Bible study group, and other specific needs I've become aware of.

Usually by the time I'm parking at work or the airport, I'm about prayed out. When I get to my seat on the plane or the parking lot at work, I will whip out my Bible and read a chapter or two in the New Testament, a chapter or two in the Old, and then work on the verses I'm memorizing. About this time the plane has reached the "10 minutes or 10,000 feet" announcement, my laptop comes up, and I type for the entire flight.

I do have a bad habit of sometimes, when I finish my Bible reading on the plane, sticking my Bible into the back pocket of the seat in front of me and forgetting it. There it remains after I've gotten off the flight. I "distribute" about one or two Bibles a year this way. In fact, I now write in my travel Bible, "If found, please keep it, God wants you to have his Word. Pat."

I also recommend a regular regimen of Bible memorization. If you have any doubts about the Bible's view on memorization, read Psalm 119, particularly verse 11:

I have hidden your word in my heart that I might not sin against you.

Of course, there are numerous overused excuses for not memorizing Scripture. I can't memorize, or I don't have time. I do it and later forget them all. I'm too old. However, in just a few minutes a day you can start to build a repertoire of verses you can utilize for the entirety of your Christian walk.

Typically, I spend about five minutes at the end of my devotion time on memorization. I usually work on two to three verses at a time. I read them over several times, then try doing a few phrases from memory. Next I try a few whole verses and so on. Often I'll try to find little hints in the passage, like taking the first letters of key words and using that sequence to help prompt me through the passage.

The next day, I'll come back and work on these verses again. I'll keep working on them until I have them mastered. Typically, in a week or so I'll have pretty well nailed a few verses. After memorizing a new section of Scripture—and this is most important—I'll then spend the next week or two reviewing all the passages I've already memorized.

Work your way through your entire portfolio of verses, taking time to review them all. Brush up on any trouble spots and keep them all fresh in your mind. After you've done so, start again with a couple of new verses. Work on them for a week or two (or three, depending on the length of the passage) until you've mastered them, and then go through a fresh cycle of reviewing the passages you already have memorized. You might also find other ways to review them. You might write them on three-by-five inch index cards and review them while driving. Or you could print them in large type and review them while on your exercise machine. You might tape them to your bathroom window or stick them in your car and practice at red lights. Take those spare couple of minutes here and there and use them to review and refresh your memory, and voila, you'll soon have a collection of twenty, thirty, fifty or more verses you've committed to memory.

This cycle of repeated review I find essential to keep building a repertoire and not just learning and forgetting. Of course, there is also the question of what verses to memorize. It's all God's Word, so none of it is bad. Generally, take verses that speak especially powerfully to you. Choose passages that might be helpful in areas where you want to focus your spiritual growth. Finally, choose verses that can help you battle specific areas of sin. Just to help get started, you might begin with verses that are already familiar to you. I'd also encourage you to pick one translation and stick to it. While reading from different versions is great and often provides insight, the minor wording differences will frustrate your attempts to build a repertoire. My current repertoire is listed here. Maybe you'll find some of these you would like to add to your own: Job 31:1; Psalm 23:1-6; Malachi 6:6-8; Matthew 4:1-16; John 1:1-18; Romans 3:21-24; 12:1-2; Colossians 3:23-24; 13:1-13; 1 Peter 1:1-9; 2 Peter 1:5-11; and Revelation 3:15-16; 21:1-7.

Generally, I find that some of my best times of prayer and praise are when I'm driving to and from work or the airport. I turn off the radio, which often has little redeeming value, and turn myself on to God. What a great way to spend that idle time as I travel to and fro. I refrain from closing my eyes, however.

Recently I was going to speak at a "Timeout" conference, but my flight takeoff was delayed due to a low cloud ceiling in San Francisco. Then we had the opportunity to circle for half an hour as air traffic was slowed and just one runway was in use. By the time we were finally given clearance to land, despite my mad dash from one wing of the airport to another, I missed my connection to the commuter flight to Monterey.

I decided to make the almost three-hour drive from San Francisco down to Monterey in a rental car, starting at about 11:30 P.M. I know I can fall asleep while driving pretty easily, so I found myself a huge cup of coffee and started singing loud and long as soon as I got in the car. I sang just about every hymn and praise song I could remember. Then I prayed aloud. Then I sang some more. For some reason the hymn "Great is Thy Faithfulness" kept coming to mind, and I probably sang it thirty times that night.

After I had been driving for almost two hours, I turned off highway 101 onto the connecting highway and, just to make it a perfect trip, I hit road construction. At 1:30 A.M. I had the opportunity to park and watch paving trucks go to and fro for fifteen minutes. I started asking God rather firmly what else he was trying to teach me that evening. But the lesson is that in our busy schedules, we can take those unexpected events and use them to God's glory. Instead of becoming painful memories, they can be opportunities to draw closer to our heavenly Father. While I was a physically tired the next morning, I was spiritually recharged like I hadn't been for weeks.

Finally, I encourage my family to do likewise. I regularly ask each of my children how they are doing and what they are reading in their devotion times. What are they learning through their personal time in the Word? Do they have questions that I might help them to understand? When I ask about what they are studying, I will also tell them what I'm reading and learning. I encourage them to ask me about my devotions as well. This idea of mutual accountability with your children can be powerful in both your lives.

CHURCH

One of the areas where we demonstrate our commitment to God is through the church and our active participation there. As Christ departed this earth, he left behind three primary institutions to guide all of mankind into a relationship with the Father: his Word (John 1:1), his Spirit (John 14:15-17), and his church (Matt. 16:18).

Throughout the mission trips of Paul and the other apostles recorded in the Book of Acts, we see them establishing the local church as the structured place for the Christians to gather, proclaim the Word, and develop relationships for support and accountability:

> Paul and Barnabas appointed elders for them in each church and, with prayer and fasting, committed them to the Lord, in whom they had put their trust. (Acts 14:23)

As we see in consistent references throughout the New Testament, the church became the basic unit of Christianity (Matt. 16:18; Acts 8:1-3; Acts 9:31; Acts 11:22).

Finally, we see an admonition by the writer of Hebrews that we should never give up the meeting together of believers. This was the place, the mechanism for his people to constantly come together to encourage one another.

> Let us not give up meeting together, as some are in the habit of doing, but let us encourage one another—and all the more as you see the Day approaching. (Hebrews 10:25)

The practical question, however, is what should we do with respect to the church as busy individuals with far too many priorities on our respective plates? First, the Hebrews passage above establishes the requirement of all believers to participate regularly in a church. I find no basis for Easter—and Christmas—only Christians. I also find no basis for substituting individual worship "wherever you find God." The church is the gathering place for teaching, proclaiming the Word, publicly declaring God's praises, mutual accountability, and corporate worship.

We must not simply slide in the back of the church around the end of the first hymn and slip out just prior to the altar call, either. The church was established as the command center for Christ's work on earth. The church is the place for teaching and instruction in the truth (Acts 2:42). It's the place for prayer needs of the body to be lifted up as a group before the Father (Acts 12:12). It's also the place for the gathering of finances to support needs of believers both locally and abroad (2 Cor. 8:19). It is the place where missionaries were set apart and sent out (Acts 13). It's the place where matters of doctrine were discussed (Acts 15:4-7). It's also the location for new believers to make their public confessions (Acts 2:41).

Based on this and many other references throughout the New Testament, I see one's relationship with God being demonstrated through active participation in the church. This could mean teaching and preaching, missions work, leadership, taking the offering and serving communion, as a prayer warrior, in support of the elderly, serving as a deacon or elder, maintenance of the church properties, and so on.

Personally, I am an elder in our congregation. Every Monday morning we have an elder prayer time for the congregation where for an hour or two we lift up specifically each and every prayer request from that week's service. All the elders are to regularly be calling on those in our respective shepherding groups. I also periodically teach classes and occasionally preach on Sunday mornings.

Linda and I have had a Bible study in our home for many years (though we currently hold it at the church building). I lead or co-lead the study. Except for the first year when we moved to Oregon and were getting acquainted with the area and finding a church home, we've had a Bible study in our home for almost the entirety of our twenty years of marriage. We have found this to be a great time of weekly fellowship. We've developed some deep friendships that now span many states as people have moved to different locations over the years. Finally, we've seen several come to Christ through this weekly time of studying God's Word.

If you are not in a study, consider it carefully. If you are in one, consider leading one. Of course, with my travel schedule I can't lead a study every week. I'm blessed to have a co-teacher who fills in for me—sometimes on a moment's notice—when a flight gets delayed or canceled, or a special event pops up. (When I didn't make study for several weeks in a row, I didn't appreciate the introduction as a visitor and the guest lecturer at the next study.)

On the other end of the spectrum, church tasks can become nothing but another set of overwhelming and endless activities. We can so easily lose sight of our relationship with the Father as we zealously pursue them, just like the religious leaders of Jesus' day. This focus brought a startling strong rebuke from Christ:

> Everything they do is done for men to see: They make their phylacteries wide and the tassels on their garments long. (Matt. 23:5)

Our church work can literally consume all the time we have for God. As Martha did in her time with Jesus, we can lose sight of the Savior (Luke 10:38-42). Church activities cannot replace a relationship with Christ, but they can displace it.

As an elder at my church, for example, I was responsible to keep in touch with and pray for about 25 families. Given my other demands, I found this overwhelming and ultimately impossible. My church service became a source of anxiety and guilt. Other elders felt the same. I'm happy to say we eventually found a solution that involved recruiting, training, and empowering some under-shepherds. But that was a Martha-like case where for a time, serving God became a burden that crushed all the joy.

With that caveat, however, maintaining a healthy balance as in all things, putting God first in our lives must include an active church life.

Finances

Throughout the gospels, we see Jesus talking frequently about money. We see that how we handle finances is critically important to our Savior (Luke 16:15). He emphasizes how our finances can become a distraction or a replacement for our relationship with God (Matt. 6:24). He addresses the manner in which we acquire money (Luke 3:14). He teaches on indebtedness (Luke 7:42-43). How we give to the Lord's work is critically important as well (Mark 12:41-44). He addresses sensitive issues like taxation (Matt. 17:24-27). He also addresses how we use and invest our finances (Mark 14:5; Matt. 25:15; Luke 19:13). One cannot finish a thoughtful reading of the Gospels and the remainder of the New Testament without realizing that to Christ and the church, how we handle money is clearly a part of our relationship with the Father. If we are going to have God as our first priority, we will handle our finances in a manner consistent with biblical truths.

I would suggest a few principles that can guide our handling of finances. We'll cover the first three of these here and a fourth in chapter 5. Moving from:
1.   Tithe to Sacrifice
2.   Debt to Inheritance
3.   Giving to Blessing
4.   Controversy to Agreement

From Tithe to Sacrifice

I've always appreciated the life and preaching of John Wesley, the great English evangelist who both authored and subsequently delivered countless sermons as he rode from town to town. His saddle, equipped with a bookshelf so he could study while he rode, remains as evidence of his dedication. He made three interesting, if not surprising, points on finances: Make all you can, Save all you can and finally, Give all you can.

Make all you can. Work hard and seek to be a successful, great employee who is rewarded suitably (Chapter 6). We shouldn't be ashamed to receive God's blessing into our lives.

Save all you can. Be frugal. Carefully plan your finances and budget (Luke 14:28); do a great job with your investments, gifts, and talents (Matt. 25:14-30). Linda and I began developing a budget from the outset of our marriage. We have been carefully planning our investments and developing an inheritance for our children and grandchildren.

Finally, Give all you can. One purpose of both earning and saving is to be able to give generously to the Lord's work. It is discouraging to see statistics showing that believers of all faiths give only a marginally higher percentage of their income to charities than do those who claim no association with any faith (2.5 percent vs. 2.2 percent). Further, those from wealthy, industrialized nations are only modestly more charitable than those from developing countries. This level of giving is so low it's startling.

If we use the Old Testament tithe of 10 percent as a starting point for giving, we fall far short. Further, we see the New Testament taking the Old Testament guidelines and turning them into more powerful principles for Christian living (1 Tim. 6:18; Acts 2:42-47, and 2 Cor. 9:11). Thus, we'd expect even greater giving under the New Covenant than the Old. Instead, however, our freedom from the Old Testament law may have become an excuse for selfishness and materialism.

> You will be made rich in every way so that you can be gen-
> erous on every occasion, and through us your generosity
> will result in thanksgiving to God. (2 Cor. 9:11)

The verse quoted above can be taken to apply to both physical riches and spiritual matters. The same Greek root word is used for clearly financial matters as well as spiritual matters in the New Testament. From this I'd suggest a principle that results from holding God as our first priority:

> *Give an increasing percentage of all we make to charity*
> *and the work of the Lord.*

As we both mature in the faith and increase our financial well-being over the course of our lives, we need to become increasingly focused on applying our wealth to his kingdom and purposes. Apply this principle and amazing things can begin to occur. Imagine how God can bless you if you are consistently pouring your finances back into his work.

Maybe you're not used to giving regularly, however. You might even be struggling to make ends meet. Giving 10 percent of your income back to God may seem impossible. In such a case, let me suggest you start giving just 1 percent and see what happens. Make that the first check you write each month. I believe you'll find God faithful to reward that step of faith by supplying all your needs.

From there, as God prospers you, you can add another percentage point to your giving each year. When you do that, as Linda and I have, you'll see God's blessings in your life in ever increasing ways. Eventually, you can be giving 20 percent, 30 percent, and even more to his work. Our family goal is to get to where we're giving more than half our income to the Lord.

As you can see from my personal mission statement in chapter 2, Linda and I aim to increase our giving every year. Look specifically at Goal #8:

> Give an increasing portion of all I earn to charity: church, missions and other Christian organizations.

This is meant mathematically as it is written, every year we give an increasing percentage of our total gross income to charities. While your mission statement is an entirely personal matter, I'd sure like yours to include this one. It would be great to give God the opportunity to bless your life with the overflowing abundance that comes from a giver's heart.

Giving our money is only the beginning of our sacrificial offering to God's work, however. We need to be actively involved in the ministries we support, investigating them carefully before we give. Linda and I discuss, prayerfully consider and carefully study charities before we give to them. We understand the mission and work of the institution and also have developed a level of personal relationship with the individuals involved.

We support several missionaries in Kenya, for example. During our recent sabbatical and vacation, we visited them for several weeks. This was a great time of visiting our friends but also an opportunity to participate in the work firsthand. We were greatly encouraged to be able to teach and meet with the many new believers in northern Kenya.

We also need to follow our giving with our thoughts and prayers. Do you stay actively involved with the ministries you support? Are you certain your finances are being used in the manner you expect? Do you know the current needs of the ministry? Do you continue to uphold these charities and ministries in regular prayer?

Debt to Inheritance

The top 15 percent of the world's population consumes 75 percent of all goods and services. A stunning one third of the world's population lives on less than $1000 per year.[3] Despite the enormous wealth of the United States and the other more developed countries, however, being the most prosperous isn't sufficient; we are also the greatest debtors on earth. The insatiable hunger of materialism forever cries for more, demanding we seek greater and greater indebtedness.

The Bible speaks clearly regarding debt—don't do it. Debt was harshly discouraged under Mosaic law, as interest or any form of indebtedness to other Israelites was forbidden (Prov. 28:8; Ezek. 18:8, 13, 17; Ezek. 22:12; Ps. 15:5). All debts were to be cancelled in the year of Jubilee (Deut. 15:1-11). We see that the debtor became enslaved in one manner or another to the debt holder, leading to long-term moral or spiritual decay.

> If you lack the means to pay, your very bed will be snatched from under you. (Prov. 22:27)

> Do not charge your brother interest, whether on money or food or anything else that may earn interest. You may charge a foreigner interest, but not a brother Israelite, so that the LORD your God may bless you in everything you put your hand to in the land you are entering to possess. (Deut. 23:19-20)

In contrast, Scripture encourages a lifestyle marked by freedom from all manner of debt, minimizing our concern for financial needs, and preparing an inheritance for the generations to come.

> For where your treasure is, there your heart will be also. (Matt. 6:21)

> Wisdom, like an inheritance, is a good thing and benefits those who see the sun. (Eccl. 7:11)

> A good man leaves an inheritance for his children's children, but a sinner's wealth is stored up for the righteous. (Prov. 13:22)

While this may sound easy, we know that it's difficult to live consistently in this manner. But if credit cards give you difficulty, cut them up and discard them before they lead you further into misery. If you have difficulty sticking to your budget, establish a system where each month you first take out all the money required for household expenses—food, savings, charities and so on. Apply them to the budget items before using any funds for discretionary spending. I'd also suggest you study and apply some of the many fine materials written on the Christian's finances.

I have a close friend who, as we have studied and met, has seen the need to simplify his financial state and move to the point where his wife no longer needs to work outside the home. They are shedding possessions, selling rental homes and other possessions, and putting themselves on a path that will steadily move them closer to freedom from debt. Another friend, realizing he couldn't give a consistent offering to the Lord's work, is planning to decrease the size of his mortgage by moving to a smaller home. I applaud the efforts of both men. They are making and carrying out tough decisions to move from debt to inheritance.

Some financial writers suggest that having a mortgage is okay, if not recommended. Not only do you garner a physical asset, the home, but you also get the benefit of the tax write-off. Certainly, a mortgage is far superior financially to paying rent, which offers no long-term financial reward. Further, for most, a mortgage is the only possible way to ever own a home.

However, some continue even further and argue that a mortgage is a great investment due to the tax write-off you receive. While you can run the numbers for your own situation you'll probably find that you come out an interest point or two ahead if you use a mortgage as an investment compared to most other low-risk investments. However, I believe strongly that the biblical principle of "no debt" should take precedence over the potential for a mere point or two of financial gain in elongating or even increasing your mortgage.

Thus, while a mortgage is a clear requirement for most, I'd challenge you to get out of debt, all of it, including your mortgage. Of course, for a mortgage, this could take quite a number of years. Get started anyway. Maybe you can increase your monthly payment by just a few percentage points. While this may not sound too exciting, you will begin to whittle away the years of that mortgage rather quickly. Increasing your monthly payment just 10 percent could take seven years or 23 percent off the duration of a 30-year mortgage. Increasing your payments just 15 percent could take almost ten years or 30 percent off the duration of a 30-year mortgage.

Linda and I started paying extra on our 30-year mortgage just a couple of years after our marriage and our first mortgage began. We increased our payments by 10 percent, then 15 percent, and 25 percent as our financial blessings allowed. We then refinanced our remaining mortgage when interest rates allowed us to move to a 15-year loan for a better interest rate. After moving to a new location, we again took out a 15-year loan. We were excited about being entirely out of debt, and we immediately began paying off our new mortgage more rapidly as well. Today I'm proud to say we have no mortgage.

Imagine a conversation with your spouse in a few years that might go something like this. "Dear, we have absolutely no debt. The house is paid for, and we have saved up finances sufficient for us to live a modest but comfortable life should either of us be unable to provide any longer for our household. We've left a biblical inheritance for our children and their children as well."

Wow, what a powerful statement! Imagine the anniversary celebration where you could burn your mortgage papers, celebrating the end of your indebtedness. While for most this will be a long, slow process, such a commitment will yield incredible fruits in this life and in the one to come.

Giving to Blessing

Most of us, particularly men, are excited about the potential for a prize or reward. Maybe it's a track event where we're focused on winning the medal or trophy. Maybe in fishing we're out to catch the trophy fish. Maybe we're working to take a few strokes off our golf score and be the best in our foursome. Maybe in our work we're eager to win an award, earn a promotion, or receive a raise. God made us such that we look forward to prizes or gifts. We shouldn't be ashamed to say we are eager for the prize or the rewards we are promised.

Personally, I'm very goal oriented. I'm out to win the prize. I'm eagerly looking forward to the blessings that God promised for a lifestyle of consistent and faithful giving to his work.

> Remember this: Whoever sows sparingly will also reap sparingly, and whoever sows generously will also reap generously. . . . Now he who supplies seed to the sower and

bread for food will also supply and increase your store of seed and will enlarge the harvest of your righteousness. You will be made rich in every way so that you can be generous on every occasion, and through us your generosity will result in thanksgiving to God. (2 Cor. 9:6, 10-11)

Give, and it will be given to you. A good measure, pressed down, shaken together and running over, will be poured into your lap. For with the measure you use, it will be measured to you. (Luke 6:38)

Some read these passages and conclude they offer an entirely spiritual benefit. I heartily agree that you will be blessed spiritually by a life of consistent and increasing giving to God's work. I receive a blessing every time the missionaries we support report progress and new believers from their ministry. I receive a blessing every time the church planting organization we support launches a new congregation. Every time a new member joins our church, I also receive a blessing.

However, from reading the context of those passages and from the Greek words used, there is no basis for a strictly spiritual interpretation. I've heard and read countless stories of people giving in faith, only to be rewarded with near immediate "surprises" from God's generosity meeting their physical needs. You receive blessings now and in the future, both spiritual and physical, for a life of faithful stewardship.

Also, God understands how finances work, and if the inflow is decreasing, the outflow can't continue to increase. Some have taken from these verses what is called the law of the harvest[4]:
• You reap after you sow.
• You reap what you sow.
• You reap more than you sow.
First comes your confidence in God to provide for your needs as you give. You cannot expect a blessing in response to greed or a love for money (1 Tim. 6:9-10, Titus 3:14). Blessings come as a result of our love for the Father and our generosity for his kingdom and its work on earth.

Second, you reap of the kind you sow. Did you sow abundantly or sparingly? Did you sow with a spirit of generosity and sacrifice as we saw with the widow in Mark 12:42-44?

Finally, you receive more than you sow. Your investments into kingdom work will be rewarded with blessings that continue to multiply. It truly is more blessed to give than to receive (Acts 20:35). As God challenges us through the prophet Malachi:

> "Bring the whole tithe into the storehouse, that there may be food in my house. Test me in this," says the LORD Almighty, "and see if I will not throw open the floodgates of heaven and pour out so much blessing that you will not have room enough for it." (Mal. 3:10)

In summary, we've covered three of four principles on godly finances, with the fourth to come in chapter 5:

1. Tithe to Sacrifice: Give an increasing percentage of all you have to charity.

2. Debt to Inheritance: Commit today to cease from all kinds of debt and pursue an inheritance for your children and grandchildren.

3. Giving to Blessing: Look forward to the rewards of a life of godly stewardship.

4. Controversy to Agreement (to be covered in chapter 5)

To live a balanced life and succeed in our juggling act, we need to place God as our first priority. This will be seen in our daily time with him. We will, as we've done on several topics in this chapter, apply the truth of his Word directly to our daily lives. We'll be regular and active in his body, the church. Finally, we will place the critical matter of our finances in submission to him.

Chapter 3 Q&A

1. How can you make and keep God your number one priority in life?

2. Do you find your religious regimen ever getting to the point where it is little more than a daily routine? How can you put more of yourself into your personal devotions and prayer?

3. Is it wise for someone who travels heavily or puts in late nights

at work to commit to leading a weekly Bible study? How can you fit your home Bible study into an already taxing schedule?

4. How can you make your finances reflect God as the highest priority in your life?

5. How do you deal with work assigned to you on a Sunday?

CHAPTER 4

Prioritize Family Time

Some close friends of our family and members of our church, Lee
and Anne Marie, decided they had been led by God to take their
family to the mission field. After over a year of preparation they were
just about ready to leave in January of '98 and make the long journey
to begin their first term. Micah, our youngest, was seven years old at
the time they were preparing to depart. He announced to us one day
with bold confidence, "When I grow up, I want to be a missionary to
Kenya!" Linda and I figured that was like a kid saying, "I want to be a
firefighter" and that he'd grow out of it. So, we smiled in affirmation
and kept our doubts to ourselves. Recently, however, on my every-
seven-years sabbatical from Intel, we made a trip as a family that
included three weeks in Kenya. We visited missionary friends working
with the Turkana people in the desolate, drought-stricken northern part
of the country, just below the Sahara.

At the end of that time, Micah said, "Thanks, Mom and Dad, for
bringing us here. I really appreciate it. And I still want to be a missionary to Kenya!" In fact, he's already planning our next family vacation
to Kenya; and he expects us to make this sojourn every year or two
until he's permanently on the mission field.

That experience demonstrates the value of two things: making time
to help your children develop a heart for God, and making time for
family vacations. As you'll see in this chapter, I didn't always do a
good job with such things.

Deuteronomy 6:5-9 says:

> Love the LORD your God with all your heart and with all
> your soul and with all your strength. These commandments
> that I give you today are to be upon your hearts. Impress

them on your children. Talk about them when you sit at
home and when you walk along the road, when you lie
down and when you get up. Tie them as symbols on your
hands and bind them on your foreheads. Write them on the
doorframes of your houses and on your gates.

As I've read and studied this passage of Scripture over the years,
I've grown in both excitement and passion for it. Read it again and let
the words of Moses just fill your heart. Let your eyes well with tears as
you see how passionate God is for His Word—how He desires that it
be affirmed by parents and embedded into the lives of their children.

Over many generations, this passage led to the development of the
phylactery, which is handed down by Orthodox Jews to this day as the
outward symbol of the Word of God in their lives. They literally bind
pouches holding Scriptures to their hands and foreheads as visible and
physical evidence of their love for God's Word. Oh, the love and passion for God's Word the author intended for us to possess. How vital
he realized it was for this passion to be handed from parents to their
children.

While most of you reading this are probably not of Jewish descent,
I'd challenge you to consider this passage with the same passion as
Moses intended. What are your family beliefs and practices, and how
will you pass them to the next generation? What are your morals and
ethical standards, and how will your family learn to hold these true and
critical for their life's work?

In our interconnected, real-time communicating world we are bom-
barded with a diverse set of choices; people can choose from an almost
infinite pool of lifestyles and religious and philosophic frameworks. As
our children are confronted with this dizzying array, our job is not to
simply offer up a full a la carte menu of the alternatives. No, we parents need to develop in our children a solid framework and understanding of our beliefs and traditions, working with them to develop their
own personal beliefs, which will govern them for the remainder of
their lives. Further, we need to model for them those values and con-
victions in the best classroom of all—our daily lives.

In this chapter we'll explore some tools to help you find time to
make that kind of impact in your children's lives.

Breakfast 1-on-1

About thirteen or fourteen years ago, when our daughter Elizabeth was just five years old, I started a practice of taking her out for breakfast each month. As the boys came along, I then had two, then three, and now four kids to take to monthly breakfast. I now have breakfast with one of the kids every week on a rotating basis. It used to be even a cheap way to have some special one-on-one time with each of them. We would usually share a breakfast, which they would choose and which made it even more enjoyable. As the kids have gotten older, however, they refuse to share with me anymore. Instead they demand their own breakfast and part of mine as well.

Over the years, the kids have really grown to look forward to these times. It's our special one-on-one time. When I return home with the designated child of the morning, the siblings will always say, "Where did you go?" and "What did you have?" . . . "You're lucky it was your turn." Sometimes, I'll drop the child off at school after breakfast on my way to work, which makes it even more special.

Of course, with a busy travel schedule, I don't make breakfasts happen each week. But I have asked my secretary to both schedule and prioritize my breakfast meetings with the kids. Sometimes it takes a bit of juggling, but generally, we get them scheduled in. When I started doing this, I had a simple thought in mind: Maybe if I start young just talking with them, it will be enough of a habit that, when they hit those rough teenage years, we will have at least some venue for continued conversation.

Our breakfast agenda is pretty simple. I only require a formal, written agenda with minutes from our last breakfast, updates on the action items agreed upon at our last meeting, and a new and proposed specific list of topics for this one.

Just kidding. The real agenda is whatever the kids want to talk about. I will bring a topic that I'll usually (but not always) bring up somewhere in the conversation. This might be an issue at home, something that's on my heart about them, a Scripture or a spiritual topic. We'll always discuss how school is going, how they are doing spiritually, and anything troubling them.

As the kids have gotten older, they have started to store up questions or issues that they want to discuss. Sometimes it's stuff related to homework. Other times, they want to discuss items related to their spiritual life. Recently, my daughter had three or four Scripture passages she was having trouble understanding. I felt like I was on a Bible Trivia show; they were tough passages. I am so proud to see them looking forward to this time and planning how they can take advantage of it.

In the many years I've been doing this, it is rare that a child doesn't want to take his turn. Occasionally, one would give me an "I'm too tired." If so, I would just go to the next kid in the rotation; and with four to choose from, I've only had one instance in twelve years where I couldn't get anyone to do breakfast with good old Dad. Even so, as my kids move into the later teen years—with more activities of their own and their increasing desire to sleep in—I'm tending to hear a few more no-thank-yous.

I also try every weekend to spend time one-on-one with each kid. This could be sitting on my lap reading a book, playing basketball, playing a board game, playing cards, helping with homework, doing some chores together, playing racquetball or tennis, or just sitting and talking about school or sports. On Sunday afternoon or evening, before the weekend is over and another frantic week begins, I do a quick mental checklist and ask myself, have I spent time with each of them? Have I had a chance just to connect with all of them individually? If not, I'll quickly try to correct my oversight and ask what they'd like to do.

Some weekends I'll start Friday night 200 E-mails behind and start Monday morning 300 behind. While I then feel an incredible burden of work and responsibilities on Monday morning, I'm also confident I've kept my priorities in the right places all weekend long.

Through these times with my kids, my goal is to learn to know my children. What are their unique character qualities? What do they like and enjoy? What are their areas of weakness for which I need to be praying? How are they uniquely gifted by God? As the Proverb indicates,

> Train a child in the way he should go, and when he is old
> he will not turn from it. (Prov. 22:6)

Note, this says "in the way he should go," not the way you've decided he should go. Darby's translation gives a bit more insight: "according to the tenor of his way." This indicates a certain bent or natural inclination unique to each child. Maybe you love football and your son loves music. Should you force him into your tenor and require him to play football, or learn to love and encourage his enjoyment for music and look forward to his concerts and recitals? Should your career or family business become his, or should you learn his bent to help him choose a profession that uniquely matches his God-given gifts and talents?

I've enjoyed trying to guess what sports or musical instrument each of our children might like based on his or her character qualities. I've also enjoyed trying to guess their potential professions based on their giftedness. I've prayed specifically for insights into how to raise and encourage them.

I recall recently a family camp weekend where Michael Smalley was the speaker. As a Christian psychologist, he had us take a personality test, and he subsequently encouraged us to have our children do likewise. I thought I had studied our children pretty well, but while I could predict the results accurately for my other three kids, I couldn't tell where Josiah would show up. When I saw his results, I went, "Wow!" All of the sudden I saw how his naturally quiet personality was hiding some strong leadership characteristics. Further, this explained several areas where I was struggling with him and didn't understand why we were having these conflicts. It was exciting to realize the source of the conflict and suddenly have new insights into how to improve our relationship.

Family Vacations

As I've already admitted, I tend to work long and hard. It should come as no surprise that in the past I have viewed taking vacations as entirely discretionary. In the first ten years of my career at Intel, I averaged less than one week a year of vacation. Being so busy with school, I almost always found myself with more than I could hope to accomplish at work. Besides, I loved what I was doing at work and school. So why would I stop and go off to do something boring like rest and relax?

Then Linda sat me down and explained that while I may not need those things called vacation times, the family needed me on vacation. It was imperative that we spend that time together and build those memories that we will share for years to come.

Well, she was right. As Linda will resoundingly affirm, it's not often when she's right that I will agree without hesitation, but this was one of those times. Since that talk our family has not missed a single day of vacation to which I am entitled.

We try to make a big deal out of our vacations. We plan and talk about them considerably as a family. We take big trips and small. In fact, I did a good amount of the editing of this book while taking my third sabbatical from Intel. We traveled through Europe, including London, Paris, Switzerland, Germany, and Austria, then spent three weeks in Kenya (the visit mentioned at the start of this chapter).

We had a wonderful time seeing these many countries, cities, and cultures as well as visiting several missionary friends in Kenya and going on several safaris. We followed this with family time at our vacation home, as well as a camping trip. Two years ago we did a trip to Disney World, the Caicos Islands in the Caribbean, and some time at a family reunion on the East Coast. The kids consider this one of our best vacations ever.

Other years we've traveled to national parks or to the East Coast for time with my parents. On other occasions, Linda and I have had romantic trips for just the two of us to Thailand, Australia, and Hawaii.

We've also tried to carve more vacation time out of our normal routine. We will spend a long weekend or school breaks skiing or at the beach. Three years ago, we purchased a vacation home as a place to develop more of those family memories. It gives us even more opportunities to get away as a family or with a few of the kids' friends.

Every spring break we go skiing. As soon as the school calendar comes out, I'll have my secretary start marking these three- and four-day weekends off on my calendar. Sometimes I need to work on those days from our vacation home, but we still get substantially more family time in as a result of just being away.

While family time is always at a premium, with planning you'll be amazed at how much togetherness you can squeeze in. Add a strong effort to protect those special times and you'll start to build tremendous family memories.

If you haven't yet gotten into the habit of making family vacations a priority, I'd challenge you to begin doing so.

Date your Spouse

I'm pleasantly surprised when I talk to people who regularly date their spouses. I'm also astonished at the number of people I talk to who can't remember the last time they and their spouses had a date. Too many times, couples have allowed their entire focus to shift to their children. They invest all their finances, all their time, and all their emotional energy in their children. Of course, children need huge quantities of all three. However, we must give our marriages even higher priority than our relationships with our children.

Only from a strong marriage comes a strong family. A strong marriage establishes a foundation for your home, in which to raise your children. The most recent census data, however, showed a continuing decline in households with both the mother and a father of the children—now less than 25 percent of all homes in the United States. Obviously, far too many people have failed to prioritize the relationship with their spouses.

The marriage bond must be held as our most-important human relationship. In Genesis we see this powerful command:

> For this reason, a man will leave his father and mother and
> be united to his wife, and they will become one flesh. (Gen.
> 2:24)

I like to choose slightly different words for each of the three commands we see there. They create a nice rhythmic trio that make the commands more memorable:

1. A man shall leave his father and mother. This is the point in his life when he severs the cords of dependency he has had with his parents.

2. He is to cleave to his wife. He should exchange the dependent relationship with his parents for an interdependent relationship with his wife.

3. Finally, they shall weave their lives together, becoming one flesh. They are to meld their lives into a single entity, intertwining their values, activities and goals. [5]

I suggest you and your spouse consider this model carefully: Leave, Cleave, and Weave. Lacking this focus on the marriage bond leaves the entire family structure on shifting sand. Soon those children will begin to leave the nest and voilà, you will be living with a stranger. You will have lost any semblance of an intimate relationship with this one called your spouse.

At one point, Linda was becoming extremely busy with the children. This wasn't too surprising, with four children and their many needs combined with my hectic travel schedule. In fact, this was almost to be expected. Feeling uneasy, however, about a few instances where it felt as if she had prioritized the kids above everything else, including me, I questioned her one evening: "Linda, am I more important to you than the kids?" It was a difficult but important conversation, as both of us realized that we were letting our precious children squeeze between us.

We decided then and there that we couldn't allow that to occur and began making some priority choices. We made it a point to hug and kiss in front of the kids and not let them come between us when we did. We stopped letting them interrupt our conversations, even though young children always think their wants are earth-shattering crises. We also determined to stop sacrificing our times together with just the two of us.

Linda and I regularly date. While our dates are often ad hoc and spontaneous, we usually have at least one every month. Our goal is to date twice per month. When the kids were younger, dating required a lot of planning; now that they're older, it's much easier to be spontaneous.

In particular to you men reading this—just do it! Make the plans, hire the sitter, and create a special time for your wife. Of course, wives, you can't overestimate the pleasure your husband receives when you take the initiative to plan a special evening for him, even if he's reluctant to admit it.

Some of our dates are expensive, like dinner in a nice restaurant. But often we just grab a burger and go to a movie. Or we rent a video and pop our own popcorn at home. We may just go to Starbucks to talk for a while. Sometimes it's a walk around the neighborhood to get fresh air and work off the stresses of the day.

Linda and I also spend at least one weekend away each year. We call this our anniversary weekend and go to a beach house or hotel. Something like this can be so valuable for your marriage. Make these times special for you and your spouse, something that you can look forward to for weeks and then recall fondly for years afterward.

For instance, this last year I started building up the excitement weeks in advance. You might have seen those little heart confetti you can buy at some drug stores—they probably cost a whopping $1.29. Each week for three weeks in advance, I'd hide those everywhere you could imagine—in her Bible, in her checkbook, in her shoes, in her pockets, in her makeup, in her car, on her pillow, in her jacket and in her clothes drawer. Multiple times a day, she'd find them falling out from all over. She even became tired of picking them up.

For our actual weekend, I planned the location, got her roses the color of our wedding roses, and had a bottle of sparkling cider waiting in the room. I also waxed poetic with one of the love notes we men hate to write. I gave her a new video camera to record more of our family times. I was excited to make this a special weekend and convey how important she is to me.

I'm sure you can be creative and plan special times uniquely suited to your spouse's likes and tastes. You simply can't overestimate the value of these little touches and special times in helping your spouse to feel loved and appreciated.

One time several years ago, I was traveling for a week in Europe, followed by a week in Japan and Asia. In between I had a free week-end where I told Linda I would come home and spend time with her and the family. She thought I was nuts. She kept challenging me to just go to Japan and spend a day or two getting some rest. Instead, through E-mail with several of her girlfriends, I planned a surprise birthday party for her on that weekend.

I landed on Saturday morning, with her and the kids picking me up at the airport. We spent some time as a family that afternoon. That evening, I had one of Linda's girlfriends come over to watch the kids, and we went to a hotel honeymoon suite downtown, where roses were waiting for her. The next morning we went to church, followed by din-ner at a restaurant. When we arrived at the restaurant—surprise! Twenty-five of her friends were waiting to wish her a happy birthday. After the festivities, we went home, I packed for Japan and Asia, and zip, off to the airport. While it was only 30 hours at home, they were hours in which Linda felt special.

I'm often asked if I golf with business colleagues. My answer is "No, I'll start playing when I get old." My kids love to tease me about this as I slowly rack up the years, and of course, I don't want to admit that I might be aging a bit. The truth, though, is that golf takes a lot of time, particularly if you want to get good at it. I'm afraid if I get seriously started, I'll attack it with the same vengeance I do other projects—a scratch golfer or bust. Maybe when the kids are gone I can get Linda to join me. However, now the boys are showing interest, so instead of time away from family, this is becoming another activity we can do together.

From Controversy to Agreement

In chapter 3 we discussed the need to put our finances under God's leadership and manage them by his principles. We discussed three principles there, with a promise to cover a fourth in this chapter. Now that we've looked at the husband-wife relationship, we're ready to consider the idea of moving from Controversy to Agreement.

Over the years, I've seen a variety of surveys and writings on causes for divorce. In almost all of them, finances are among the big three reasons. To resolve those problems, I'd like to suggest a simple but profound cure: "Just agree."

Consider these words in the biblical book of Ephesians:

Wives, submit to your husbands as to the Lord. Now as the church submits to Christ, so also wives should submit to their husbands in everything. Husbands, love your wives, just as Christ loved the church and gave himself up for her. In this same way, husbands ought to love their wives as their own bodies. He who loves his wife loves himself. (Eph. 5:22, 24, 25, 28)

The principle taught in this passage is powerful—mutual submission. In the context of this discussion, instead of demanding your way, you and your spouse (if you're married) each need to fully agree on every aspect of your family finances.

Make every major purchase a thoughtful, prayerful consideration between the two of you. Come into full agreement on all aspects of the purchase—cost, make, model, timing and so on—before buying. If you don't agree, don't make the purchase until you do.

Some close friends told us the story of their recently married daughter and her husband. The daughter decided she needed a new car. On her own, she went out and bought one that was far more expensive than they could afford. When her husband came home, she, with gleeful naiveté, announced the purchase as if he should appreciate her initiative and self-confidence.

Well, the son-in-law needed a newer vehicle much more than his wife. Realizing his opportunity, he went out and bought an even fancier model for himself the next day. Needless to say, if one new car payment was outside their budget, two new cars certainly were. This is not what I have in mind by mutual submission.

We men have greater difficulty with mutual submission than women do. As the age-old adage says, "The difference between men and boys is the price of their toys." Maybe we really don't need that new hunting rifle, sports car, water ski boat, jet ski, ultra-lite fly rod, or off-road vehicle.

I recall a number of years ago when we had an encyclopedia salesman come to our house. I love books and the pursuit of knowledge. Not only did I want to get a set of encyclopedias ("a great investment for the kids"), but I also wanted to buy the entire set of "Great Books," many of the classic writings of the last two millenniums. Well, when the salesman came at the prearranged time, Linda had fallen ill and was lying in bed. Applying the "agree to agree on finances" principle, I kept going into the bedroom to discuss our purchase with her.

After several treks back and forth, she finally succumbed to my desires. I was thrilled and eager for the arrival of my new books. What a lousy purchase! Despite her downtrodden, ill condition, I had strong-armed Linda into agreeing with me. This single purchase has haunted me over the years as I realized I pressured her into it, particularly at a time when she wasn't feeling well. To this day we keep the "Great Books" prominently displayed in our living room, almost all of which have never been opened. They serve as a constant reminder of the need for us to agree.

Apply this principle to all forms of investment as well. Invest nothing unless you and your spouse agree entirely. I find that we men are generally more willing to take higher risks. We'd put the house at risk for the promise of a great gain. Often our wives can provide a more balanced and cautious perspective.

When we first married, Linda viewed stocks and stock options as gambling and, thus, wrong. So we didn't do anything in the stock market. With recent dramatic declines in tech stocks . . . maybe she was right. In fact, we almost allowed our first stock options to expire before exercising them. After a variety of explanations of how stocks are holdings with underlying assets of substance and value, we finally made it past the "this is gambling" conversation. We are now share-holders as one of our agreed upon areas of investments.

Apply this same principle to your discretionary and entertainment budgets. How much will you spend at work on lunches and the like, or should you take along a home-cooked meal and save a few dollars? How much should go for monthly entertainment activities? How often will you eat out, and how much will you spend on restaurants? How much, if anything, will you give to the kids in allowances or in pay-ment for chores? All of these should be agreed upon between you and your spouse.

Similarly, apply this to your charitable giving. Every place and amount should be decided in complete harmony between the two of you. Maybe you want to support a charity and your spouse isn't yet comfortable with it. Don't do it. Maybe you're convinced about the principle of continually increasing your financial giving as we dis-cussed in chapter 3, but your spouse isn't. Don't do it.

Obviously, a conflict could arise between the principles of financial obedience to God and submission to your spouse. While I don't see a clear or simple resolution, I think submission to your spouse will pro-vide a greater long-term gain. Tell your spouse of your desire to give to the charity and your belief that it's the appropriate way to honor God. However, out of submission to his or her desires, you won't make the gift. Then prayerfully take this matter to God to change your heart or your spouse's. The change that results will help both of you to grow up spiritually.

I counseled a Christian woman whose husband isn't yet a believer. The matter of giving had become a divisive issue between them. Instead of helping to draw him to Christianity, the issue was becom-ing another excuse for him to build a wall around his life. I advised her to submit to his wishes while still making clear her desires. We hope that he might eventually be won over by his wife's behavior (see 1 Pet. 3:1).

Applying this principle of mutual submission or "agree to agree" on all matters of finances can have powerful results in the husband-wife relationship. If you can't agree—don't do it. Choose a common amount and purpose for each aspect of your financial activities. After a year or two of doing this, your finances and your marriage should be in much better shape.

Of course, some of you reading this may not be married. You can still apply this principle by finding a mentor or an accountability partner. Choose someone for whose financial prowess you have a high regard, and ask the person to play the role of financial accountability associate for you. Work with that individual in building your budget. Use him or her as the one to "agree to agree" with on major financial decisions.

The second major priority of our lives is family relationships. Prioritize your bond with your mate through dating and time away for the two of you. Manage your finances with mutual agreement. Build into your life regular times with your children. While juggling is never simple, with God and family clearly and properly prioritized, you'll be ready to consider the third major priority.

Chapter 4 Q&A

1. How do you prioritize your spouse above your children and profession?

2. Are regular dates with your spouse really that necessary? Why?

3. How can you make family time a priority in your regular week- ly activities?

4. How does your spouse manage alone with the kids when you're away?

5. How would you handle a spouse who is intensely busy, gone a lot, not involved in church or family, and not responsive to your suggestions to alter his or her priorities?

6. If your spouse is an extreme workaholic or simply refuses to adjust priorities, what can you do to improve the situation?

Work Hard

At Intel, we often have two people share a job for a time; we call them "two in a box" relationships. Sometimes it's because we've merged two groups and this smoothens the transition. Other times, a job is just too big for one person. And still other times, it's a way for a senior person to develop a younger one.

At one point fairly early in my career, I was paired in a box with a seasoned manager named Mike. I was aggressive and on a fast track; he was experienced and one of the best program managers I've ever seen anywhere.

On one occasion, we were both sent an e-mail asking for specific direction on a matter I considered relatively minor. The message included a proposed course of action, and since the matter fell more on my side of the job responsibility, I shot back a quick "okay."

Shortly thereafter, I got an E-mail from Mike. "It's not okay, and you know it," he said. "It's just not that important to you, and you aren't doing your job by letting it slide."

Wow, was I rebuked! And I deserved it. Mike was spot on. I had been lazy and in a hurry to get the question out of my in box. I learned a lesson that day that I've never forgotten: I'm going to handle everything I'm responsible for to the best of my ability, even when it's not my highest priority.

As outlined so far in this book, first, develop a plan for your life. Second, prioritize your personal relationship with God and third, your family time. Having established that order to your life, you are now ready to tackle the fourth-in-importance priority, your profession or job.

I firmly believe that Christians should be the absolute best employees. We should be able to look at our work activities and with confidence before our heavenly Father and earthly employer declare, "I've given the very best I have to offer." Christians should be the hardest working of them all. Again I'd emphasize, this isn't an excuse for workaholism. However, in the hours we apply to our jobs, typically one-third or more of our entire lives, the message is simple: do your best.

Scripture clearly and repeatedly supports this perspective.

> Whatever you do, work at it with all your heart, as working for the Lord, not for men, since you know that you will receive an inheritance from the Lord as a reward. It is the Lord Christ you are serving. (Col. 3:23-24)

We see this theme communicated here and in Ephesians 4:28; 1 Thessalonians 4:11; 5:12,13; 2 Thessalonians 3:10; and in 1 Corinthians 4:12; 9:6; 15:58. I'm not a theologian, but the simple rule of letting Scripture interpret Scripture is one of the basic tenets of Bible study. In other words, if Scripture keeps repeating and elaborating on itself, listen up.

Maybe I'm an idealist, but I'd like to believe that every Christian is a great employee. That's not because Christians are superior to non-Christians. Scripture clearly directs us to "in humility consider others better than [our]selves" (Phil. 2:3).

Instead, since we have, as Colossians directs us, an "inheritance from the Lord," we can look past the day-to-day politics, disputes, personal attacks, and any other distraction and see that our ultimate reward is not a paycheck, a promotion, personal recognition, stock options, a more powerful position, or any other worldly recognition. Rather, our reward is a powerful yet simple "Well done, my good and faithful servant," from our heavenly Father as we receive that inheritance of eternal life from him.

Christians shouldn't be embarrassed or hesitant to aspire to be great, however. We should seek to gain positions of influence and use those for God's kingdom. Think of the great men of the Bible: Joseph, second in command to the greatest earthly leader of the time, Pharaoh; Moses, son of Pharaoh, leader of the Hebrew nation; Daniel, second in command to three different kings; Nehemiah, trusted advisor to his king; and David and Solomon, leaders of the greatest nation on earth in their day. Over and over we see men of God in positions of greatness and influence.

We read in the recently popularized prayer of Jabez:

> Jabez cried out to the God of Israel, "Oh, that you would bless me and enlarge my territory! Let your hand be with me, and keep me from harm so that I will be free from pain." And God granted his request. (1 Chron. 4:10)

He clearly sought the Lord's blessing on his life and possessions, but with God's hand on him, guiding his every step. I pray this prayer often: Oh Lord, enlarge my territory that I could be an increasingly powerful witness for your kingdom. Oh Lord, enlarge my possessions so that I may give greater support to the work of your kingdom here on earth. Oh Lord, use whatever position I am in at work, home, or in the community to lead people to you through my life and witness.

Balancing Work and Rest

Over my career, as described in chapter 1, I've had some intense periods of hard work. When we were completing the 80486 chip design, for example, our lives consisted of maybe eighteen-to-twenty hours on the job, go home, sleep a bit, shower and be back in six-to-eight hours for another eighteen-to-twenty hours. We were working around the clock, every day of the week.

We had committed to upper management to be done by Christmas 1988. Well, December 25th came and went, and while we were working at a feverish pace, the chip wasn't yet complete. New Year's Day came and went. We labored through January and into February. The days and hours continued to build in intensity and pressure.

One day when we were approaching the climax of tapeout, a team member came wandering into my office. As he sort of stumbled in, he muttered in fractured sentences and incomplete words about a problem with the chip. Clearly, this fellow was on the verge of burnout and needed a break, quick.

After the climax of tapeout was thankfully completed and we were waiting for the first samples back, we took immediate and drastic action. Except for a skeleton crew, we kicked people out of the building and insisted they take some well earned rest and relaxation. If they weren't part of the skeleton crew, they weren't to be found in the building for three weeks, or until the first test silicon had returned from the fabrication facility, whichever came first.

Maybe we can refer to this as "managed intensity." We need to balance periods of great focus and work, of being the best, and applying huge portions of our time to our careers, with times for rest, relaxation, family, and vacations.

Working hard while prioritizing God and family is much like the juggling act I referred to earlier. While work demands, church demands, and personal time are clamoring for our attention, the challenge and opportunity is to just do it. My wife and I have had more discussions about my schedule and time than anything else in our married life. On more than one occasion, these have developed into heated arguments.

About five years ago, we started a point system to keep track of how I'm doing. This may sound a bit crazy, but it has helped us not to debate the data but instead to move quickly to a positive discussion concerning what to do about her feeling alone or her belief that I've not been around enough recently.

Our system works like this: days I'm home before 5 P.M. , two points; days I'm home before 6:15 P.M., one point; and days after 6:15 P.M. or not home at all that evening, zero points. Weekend days away get minus one point. At the end of each month, we compare the sum of these points with the number of work days in the month. My example below is for thirteen-month period. Vacations or holidays don't count (unless, of course, I'm traveling on any of those days, in which case they count as minus one each).

	2000						2001						
	June	July	Aug	Sep	Oct	Nov	Dec	Jan	Feb	Mar	April	May	June
Home by 5:00	16	2	6	10	8	12	2	10	10	12	6	14	8
By 6:15	5	6	5	4	6	9	3	11	5	4	2	7	7
After 6:15	2	2	9	11	12	5	7	6	9	7	16	8	6
Weekend day		0	0	-1	-2				-1		-5		
Total Points	21	8	11	13	12	21	5	21	14	16	3	21	15
work days/month	22	9	18	20	22	20	11	22	19	17	21	22	11

Percentage	95%	89%	61%	65%	55%	105%	45%	95%	74%	94%	14%	95%	136%
6 mo rolling average	72%	72%	72%	73%	78%	78%	70%	71%	73%	78%	71%	70%	85%
Yearly Average	71%							85%					

before 5	2 pt
by 6:15	1 pt
after 6:15	0 pt
Weekend	-1 pt

This system has helped remove the emotion from our discussion of my time. Prior to instituting this system, we'd often have conversations something like:

Linda: "You've been gone too much lately."

Pat: "No, I've actually been home more this last month than the prior."

Linda: "No you haven't, this month has been much worse than the prior."

Pat: "Well, that's not really the case. Remember last week, I was home four out of five nights."

Linda: "But the week before you were gone four days and had some meetings on the weekend."

Pat: "No, that was last month."

Linda: "No, it wasn't."

Pat: "Yes, it was before our Mother's Day weekend celebration."

Linda: "No, . . . "

While this system is far from perfect, it puts the data in front of both of us and allows us to focus on the real issues. Maybe this was a good month for being home, but Linda didn't feel that way. Perhaps I was home more but not being helpful around the house or taking the kids to and fro and letting Linda have some well deserved quiet time. Then maybe I could adjust things and get this one from basketball practice and take that one to his hockey game and allow Linda to spend the entire evening without getting in the car. Other times, I had simply not kept a careful watch on my schedule and allowed meetings and other work to take over again.

A little over a year ago, Linda and I had a discussion as I was getting home a little later a few more nights of the week and hitting the airport tarmac a few too many times a month. I then discussed it with my spiritual mentor, Bryce (I'll talk about him more in the next chapter). Finally, Linda and I sat down to address the situation at length.

While the conversation was difficult, we've now instituted some actions to improve my time at home. I pretty strictly leave work at 5 P.M. Monday through Thursday. To get an early start on the weekend, I leave by 4 P.M. on Fridays. Linda and the kids don't care how early I start work in the morning; they are in bed anyway or getting ready for school. Typically I will get into work at 6 A.M. or sometimes even earlier to stay on top of things. Also, after the kids have gone to bed at night, it doesn't matter to them how late I stay up working. It matters an awful lot, however, how many hours I am home—really home and undistracted—between 5 P.M. and 10 P.M. during the week and on weekends. I treat those as the precious family hours they are and put great priority on being there then.

Of course, I'm still far from perfect. Sometimes I'll hide in the garage or take a swing around the block once before pulling into the driveway to finish that last important call. However, while this system is far from perfect, my scores have again been slowly climbing upward.

Work/Family Conflicts

Of course, this idea of managed intensity won't come easily, and on many occasions will come under intense pressure as you try to balance work and family time. Sometimes this pressure will come from your own desires to achieve and be successful. Other times it will arise from your boss or workplace, where you will be asked to step up to a higher level, stay late, or push out a family commitment.

A few years ago, I was in charge of a project that was to be launched at PC Expo in New York City. PC Expo typically falls in mid-June, right after the kids get out of school. Unfortunately, before this venue and date were confirmed for the product launch, we as a family had decided to take the first two weeks after school as our yearly vacation time. We had made some extensive plans, and not only would it be difficult to change them, but it would have also been a big disappointment to the rest of the family. All of a sudden, a huge conflict of family and work was underway.

To make matters worse, this was a high visibility project in the company. Further, Intel's president, Andy Grove, held a personal interest in the project. Nonetheless, living by my priorities, I decided that I would keep the commitment to my family vacation. I worked to prepare other capable folks to handle the launch in my absence.

When Andy learned of my plans, he was disappointed and communicated that displeasure on multiple occasions both privately and publicly. If you'd ever met Andy, you'd understand the intensity his communications can take. I was in the doghouse, and everyone knew it. To make matters even worse, the launch of the new category of products was less than perfect, and one of our largest customers got upset with Intel in the process. With this miscue added to my perceived sin of prioritization, my office suddenly felt like a Siberian kennel.

Clearly, part of this was my own doing in failing to have everything prepared completely, but fundamentally, I had made a firm decision to prioritize family over work. Reflecting on the period, other than better preparation, I'd make the same decisions all over again.

On many other occasions, I've chosen conference calls over flying to be face-to-face for a meeting. I'll prepare other managers to cover meetings for me. Other times I may not stay late to finish a particular project. I typically will not take calls after maybe the first twenty minutes or so while I drive home. I bow out of numerous opportunities to entertain or to spend time socializing after work. I've said no to taking on an extra project that might have helped me to win credits toward a promotion or raise.

Conflicts will come, and storms will arise. However, if you've developed a clear reputation for being a hard worker and a great employee, you can weather them. Not only will you weather them, but your character will also grow and your reputation and credibility will increase through the process. If you are intensely committed to the company's success and doing your best in all situations—even ones where you may not like your job, peers, or supervisors—you can live by your principles and still be highly successful.

On the one hand, you need to make the commitments and tradeoffs to do nothing but a great job, to engage in those periods of intensity with your total commitment and focus. Doing that, however, requires and allows you to balance those periods with times of rest and vacation.

Working hard and being a great employee over an extended period will build a stronger and stronger reputation for yourself at your place of employment. Think of it like an invisible bank account of long-term value to your employer. If you have worked hard and shown great dedication to the company, you will be well positioned to handle the turbulent times as they arise; I promise you, they will come. Practically speaking, there are always difficulties. Spiritually speaking, Satan will not allow a man or woman of principle to emerge without more than a few challenges to the person's decisions and choices.

> In fact, everyone who wants to live a godly life in Christ Jesus will be persecuted. (2 Tim. 3:12)

For instance, suppose you've been one of the top ranked employees over many years. You've gone the extra mile on programs critical to the company; you've shown unswerving ethics and consistent loyalty. Consequently, you will have created a value-account of great positive merit on your behalf. Then a situation like the vacation example above arises. While the company may not be pleased with the tradeoff you are making in this particular instance, this situation would be considered in the overall context of your employment. And your hugely positive invisible value-account easily covers this withdrawal.

Suppose, on the other hand, that you've had continual second thoughts about this company. You've done well at times, but during other periods you've had questionable performance. You've conflicted with different supervisors, doing well with some but poorly with others. You've also had accusations of inappropriate behavior or challenging the ethics of your supervisors. In this case, lacking a strong and consistent reputation for being a great employee, tough situations will be difficult if not impossible to weather. Some instance will arise where you desperately want to make good on a commitment to your family, but your value-account at work is already in a deficit. Making another withdrawal will put you firmly into bankruptcy court, jeopardizing your position or long-term career.

On two occasions following my PC Expo conflict, I was again faced with a choice between a family vacation commitment and a work commitment. In one case, our family plans were flexible. I sought but couldn't find a suitable replacement for my work commitment. Given the flexibility in the family situation, I took a day out of my vacation and kept the work commitment.

In the other instance, our family plans were set, and I again made the decision to keep that commitment. This case wasn't as visible or significant as the PC Expo example above, but it was still a visible decision to live by my priorities and put family first.

I'd encourage you not to be simply dogmatic in either direction. Applying these principles in the various circumstances you will face can be challenging. Sometimes, your choice will be clear; other times, judging whether you can afford to keep the family commitment will prove difficult, if not impossible.

Yes, we're to the point where you can clearly see the juggling act at work. Conflicts between work, family and God lie squarely in front of us. A consistent and strong reputation can carry you through many challenges. If you've made it this far, you are making strong progress toward becoming a master juggler. However, making these gray-area judgment calls requires learning, prayer, and wisdom, and a few other wise heads around you won't hurt either (the subject of our next chapter).

Chapter 5 Q&A

1. How do you handle work commitments that come into conflict with family commitments?

2. How can you manage when projects become intense and short target dates are set—when it becomes difficult to please family and friends while still being an effective employee?

3. In an environment where corruption is a way to achieve goals, how can one maintain integrity?

4. Would you continue to work hard even if you came across unethical behavior in your company?

5. A bad economy puts a lot of pressure in our work lives. Where should one draw the line in terms of commitments and responsibilities?

6. How do you see the trade-off between working to fill the pockets of another individual and earning a living for yourself?

7. How often do you review your time chart?

CHAPTER 6

Mentors

At a late stage of the 80386 design, I gave a presentation to upper level management at Intel. I had gone from being a technician to being an engineer (though still quite the junior). I managed a few technicians and had gained credibility and increasingly responsible roles within the design team. However, I was largely unknown to most of the management. I had made it past private first class, but not too much further in my career progression. At this point in time, I was directly in charge of the tapeout process for the 80386.

The point of my presentation was that because of serious, persistent problems with our computer systems, disaster loomed on the horizon. We might never be able to finish the chip. This created a buzz of controversy, but I stood by my data and assertion and insisted that we urgently escalate the matter with our mainframe supplier to get the issues resolved.

One day a week or so after this meeting, I was huddled comfortably in my office, intently working on a portion of the chip. Wrapped up in my own little world of problems, ideas, and design, it might have taken a cannon blast to bring me back to the surrounding environment. Instead, all it took was for my phone to ring.

I had absolutely no desire to be disturbed and was annoyed at this blast of bells. After several rings, which didn't stop despite my reluctance to answer, I picked up the phone and in the most annoyed, disturbed, and sarcastic voice I could muster demanded, "Who is it?"

The response was a baritone "Andy."

To which I, attempting to outdo the sarcasm of my greeting, bellowed, "Andy who?"

The response came back quickly, "Andy Grove."

I almost died. I was more flustered and embarrassed than any other time I can recall. Andy seemed undeterred, however, and described how he had been impressed by my presentation the other day. He wanted to know my career plans at the company.

After my weak reply, he began shelling me with rapid fire questions: What are your goals? What do you read? What are you studying? What do you want to be your next job? Having started in a flustered state, I could barely form adequate sentences in response.

Following a few of these interactions, he replied: "Those are lousy answers. Be in my office within two weeks with better ones."

He was right about my answers. I had been startled by his call and entirely unprepared for his line of questioning. Besides, other than "being an engineer," I hadn't considered carefully what I wanted to accomplish.

I arranged time in a couple of weeks and went with trepidation to Andy's office to discuss my career and development goals. This began an ad hoc mentoring relationship that lasted many years. As he would see weaknesses or problems in my character, or as I would be struggling with certain areas or issues, I'd get some time on his calendar, and he would offer his wealth of experience, genius, and expertise to this young and ambitious soul. (Among other things, as mentioned elsewhere, he got me to broaden my reading interests and sharpen my career goals.)

I still reflect on this experience and say, "Wow!" Andy reached numerous layers down in the organization and tapped upon me with interest. As president of the company, he was incredibly busy. Also, he was surrounded by other aspiring and capable individuals. I was humbled but also extraordinarily motivated by his interest in my career. I listened studiously to his guidance. I might question his comments, challenge them enough that I really understood, but never would I dismiss them.

Over the years, as I've emulated Andy's actions, nothing disappoints me more than someone whom you are working to mentor but who will not accept your counsel. Not that anyone should simply take a mentor's advice and implement it blindly. However, a mentor's feedback should be consumed, pondered deeply, and in most cases put into practice with specific action plans. To be mentored, you must have a teachable spirit.

> The way of a fool seems right to him, but a wise man listens to advice (Prov. 12:15).

I've been extraordinarily blessed to have some wonderful mentors and teachers in my career. I've worked with some of the finest in the industry. I've been counseled by the greatest technologist of semi-conductors, Gordon Moore, mentored by the greatest strategist, Andy Grove, guided by one of the greatest managers, Craig Barrett. I've met and worked with household names like Bill Gates, Larry Ellison, Michael Dell, and Steve Jobs. As a leader in our field, I get to inter-act with many of the best and brightest throughout the high tech industry.

Through my experience with Andy, I began to understand this idea of "mentors" in a deep and profound way. We can see it in scripture:

> Two are better than one, because they have a good return for their work: If one falls down, his friend can help him up. But pity the man who falls and has no one to help him up! Also, if two lie down together, they will keep warm. But how can one keep warm alone? Though one may be overpowered, two can defend themselves. A cord of three strands is not quickly broken. (Eccl. 4:9-12)

I love that last line: a cord of three strands is not quickly (or, in some translations, easily) broken. Sometimes events and difficulties arise that we simply don't have the capacity to handle in our own wis-dom, abilities, or strength. But through our relationships and particu-larly our mentors, we "aren't quickly broken." Jesus provided that kind of relationship to his twelve disciples, and even more intimately with his inner three. We see other examples in Scripture, like when Paul takes the great apostle Peter aside and rebukes him (Gal. 2:11). We see Paul with his band of young disciples in Timothy, Titus, and others. We see Paul working alongside Barnabas as a peer. We see him taking these individuals he's mentoring and passionately and lovingly guiding them in letter after letter of the New Testament.

In my own goals I've taken the goal of:

> #3. Assist in bringing to Christ or to a much greater degree of Christian maturity over 100 people.

While I think that's a great goal, I've recently begun to wonder if maybe a better goal would be to really influence ten in a substantive and meaningful way.

It's often beneficial to have multiple mentors in our lives. Our spiritual mentor may not be the same person we need for our career or professional mentor. We might also have certain areas of our lives where we need a mentor who is specifically strong or capable in that area.

Maybe you're struggling with how to be a better spouse; you should seek a mentor who is particularly strong in that area. Choose someone whose relationships with children and spouse are the kind you want for yourself.

Maybe you need to work on a certain skill set in your work life, like time management. You should seek a mentor who has demonstrated ability in planning and in managing his or her life with discipline and order.

Let me also encourage you to pursue at least three levels of mentoring relationships: A mentor, a peer, and a mentoree. Scripturally, you can compare this to having a Paul in your life, a Barnabas, and finally a Timothy. While a direct biblical connection might be stretching the Scripture a bit, in my own mind I equate these three with the "three strands" of Ecclesiastes 4:12.

First, you need someone you are being mentored by, like Paul was to Timothy or Titus. This should be someone you can look up to and respect. Someone who has capabilities and experiences you haven't yet experienced. Someone who's accomplished and mature in areas you desire to grow in. You also need someone who is willing and committed to investing in your life. Finally, that person needs to be eager to see you grow and succeed. For many years, this is the role that Andy Grove played in my professional career.

> But you know that Timothy has proved himself, because as a son with his father he has served with me in the work of the gospel. (Phil. 2:22)

Second, you need a peer, someone you can be a deep friend, buddy, or pal with. Paul and Barnabas had this kind of relationship. You need someone who isn't impressed by you, who is ready to tell you the truth. Someone who sees you enough to observe your successes and your mistakes and isn't afraid to tell you about them. Paul filled this role for Peter at least once. Envision this interaction as described by Paul:

> When Peter came to Antioch, I opposed him to his face, because he was clearly in the wrong. Before certain men

came from James, he used to eat with the Gentiles. But when they arrived, he began to draw back and separate himself from the Gentiles because he was afraid of those who belonged to the circumcision group. (Gal. 2:11-12)

That seems like an Intel meeting to me—not meant to create strife, but direct and very blunt when something doesn't seem quite right. Maybe you can recall a few similar instances at your place of employment.

Given my strong personality, finding a peer has been hard for me over the years. I'm not particularly open about my feelings, and I don't find many people whom I don't overwhelm and yet I trust and respect. I was saddened when one peer moved to Kenya to be a missionary. It had taken me too long to find one, and now I needed to travel halfway around the world to see him.

Third, you need someone to whom you are passing your life's experiences. Someone you can teach, tutor, and encourage. Someone in whose growing maturity you take joy.

As a manager for many years, I've picked a few people to mentor in whom I saw potential and thought they could benefit from what I've learned. I've taken great pleasure in seeing some of them making it to positions of director, vice president, or fellow. What a joy to see those you've invested into making it to positions of success and influence, knowing you helped them get there.

As I've given this talk over the years, I've been asked numerous times, how do you find a mentor, or do they find you? Well, I'm sorry to tell you that I've found no simple formula. Much of it is simply the right interpersonal chemistry. Not being a psychologist, I can't describe why some relationships work great and others don't. However, let's try to identify a few critical characteristics of a good mentor. I think there are three:

1. Trust and respect—You need someone whom you have a genuine respect for; you'll naturally value the person's opinions and what he or she has to say. You need someone you can trust—someone you are comfortable telling about your deepest feelings, sins and failures, and emotions. Similarly, for the people you are mentoring, they need that of you.

2. Character and capabilities—Your mentor should have capabilities you want to learn. If a class advertised that the teacher had

never actually done what he was going to talk about but he'd read up on it real good, would you attend? Of course not. You want to learn from a master. Similarly in your mentor, you want someone who has skill and experience in those areas where you wish to improve.

3. Time and commitment—While it may not require a huge amount of time, mentoring does demand a commitment. It might be just an hour or two every couple of months. Or you might be in a period of your life when mentoring is more critical and you need to meet much more frequently—maybe once per week.

Finding a mentor can be challenging. Sometimes, as in the case of Andy Grove with me, a mentor will seek you out. May God grant you such good fortune.

I suggest, however, that you don't just wait for someone to ask you. Go broach the subject with a person you'd like as a mentor. Say something like: "As I'm growing and learning, I see the value a mentor could play in my life. I've been impressed by what you've done with your life, and you have some skills and knowledge I could really benefit from. Can I talk with you about possibly becoming a mentor to me?"

I recall one summer several years ago when a college student doing an internship at Intel approached me in this manner. I was not only somewhat flattered, but I also gained an immediate respect for the young man. He sought to better himself, and he was eager to find people who might help. He had done his homework, knowing a good bit about me, my career, and my faith. He was also well prepared with a list of questions he wanted to discuss with me. I became quickly convinced that any time I spent with him would be a good investment of my energy.

Seeking out your Timothy is another matter. Imagine an aspiring young person getting a call from you saying something like: "I've watched you, and you have talent. I enjoy watching you grow and develop. I'd like to invest some of my life's experiences and wisdom into your life. Can we get together sometime and talk about it?" I've never heard of such a call being rebuffed, even if the two of you eventually decide you're not the right fit for each other.

Finally, how do you recruit a Barnabas? You might say something like "I could really use someone to get together with and confidentially share our concerns and weaknesses. I'd like an accountability partner who would commit to meet and pray with me periodically. I don't know if you have the time or desire for this, but if we could get together to discuss the possibility sometime, I'd really appreciate it."

As noted above, sometimes you need a mentor in a specific area of your life. You might mentor him in some ways and be mentored by him in others.

A close friend, Bryce Jessup, is the man who married Linda and me almost twenty years ago. Over the years, we have stayed in close contact. Bryce is well regarded in the area of marriage and family, and over the years I've continued to use him as a mentor in these areas. At the same time, Bryce has found me valuable as his "vision" mentor. As president of a San Jose Christian College, he needs to set a direction and paint a vision for the staff, supporters, board, and student body. I've been able to challenge him to think bigger, to see a greater God and the potential areas where God could enlarge his work. Given my business experience, I've also helped him learn how to engage with business men and include them in his work and vision. Thus, we've been mentors to each other in these different areas.

I recall one occasion a few years ago when I was serving as a board member for Bryce's college. He had me over that evening after the board meeting and, with some trepidation, asked if he could share his vision for the college. I said sure, fire away. He jumped right in and went on for five plus minutes. He described his ideas for the campus physical property, for new programs for students, and for growth in the student body. He discussed a few longer range ideas he had as well. When he finished, he eagerly asked what I thought.

With little hesitation, I gave him a single word reply: "Wimpy." I felt strongly led to challenge him to a greater and bolder vision for the college. My God was greater than the picture he was painting, and I was certain he would and could use the college in a more powerful way.

Bryce was immediately crushed and defeated by my quick and harsh critique. However, this prompting eventually led Bryce to a much more aggressive plan for the college. (The college is now committing to a physical move to a new, dramatically larger property, expectations for a broad range of new programs, and a quadrupling or more of the student body.) Today Bryce is absolutely passionate for the Lord's work, and the vision he has for the college. He's more confident than ever of God's leading and direction in his ministry. Though he has reached an age at which many would consider retirement, he's launching maybe the most productive period of his long and effective ministry. This is the kind of thing that mentors will do for each other, challenging and encouraging each other to do greater things and become greater individuals for God. While they love the other person just the way he or she is, they are eager to see the person improve and accomplish greater things professionally and spiritually.

This example also allows me to make another point. Generally, a mentor is someone you'd consider older than yourself. With age comes experience and wisdom. The Bible clearly teaches us to honor age. Don't treat age as a firm requirement, however, as you go about picking your Paul, Timothy, and Barnabas. While I won't point out how much older Bryce is than I am, it brings me a certain pleasure when he refers to me as his mentor.

As we've gone through this discussion, I've generally presented mentoring as a specific and on-going relationship. But you will find that many ad-hoc situations arise in which you might be mentored or be able to mentor someone else. One friend of mine at Intel, Will, often passes me a casual note in a meeting or a gesture when he sees me getting into difficulty. Likewise, I will advise him when I see areas in his life that he might be able to improve. On one occasion before a particularly difficult presentation, Will took me aside a few minutes beforehand and encouraged me to acknowledge the others who had participated in this material's preparation. He also cautioned me to emphasize the primary point I needed to make without getting stuck on some of the other important but potentially distracting items. The presentation went particularly well, and Will's timely advice was quite valuable.

On another occasion, I noticed that Will would become defensive at moments of great stress in meetings. His reactions would become too emotional, leading others to disregard his valuable inputs. I advised him and helped him overcome this weakness, leading to a significant increase in his effectiveness. Over the years, our casual and ad-hoc mentoring has proved valuable for both of us.

In a particularly difficult real-estate transaction, I've been advising a close friend on how he might handle the myriad of issues in both negotiations as well as legal matters. In yet another situation, I've been encouraging the head of a church planting organization to be more aggressive and take the ministry to a greater level of impact and results.

By the same token, in recent years I've been counseled in overcoming some difficulties I've had in professional interpersonal relationships. While I had taken steps to address them, the same kinds of comments had shown up in my performance reviews for probably the last fifteen years. Some specific and focused mentoring in these areas has resulted in breakthroughs that many have recognized. One person commented to me a couple of years ago, "I like the new Pat."

While some companies offer specific mentoring programs, to me the critical aspects of mentoring do not come from a program. The keys are, first, finding an individual with the right skills and interpersonal relationship; and second, your decision to better yourself based on the advice of this person.

Finally, a few words of warning are in order. A mentoring relationship is deeply personal. You'll be sharing the depths of your character, emotions, desires, and secrets. Confidentiality is crucial. That expectation and commitment to each other should be spelled out and agreed to up front. I've never been badly burned by a mentoring-related indiscretion, but some things I considered private have been spread to others.

Another potential danger is simple neglect. One or both parties just don't have the time to invest in the relationship, or maybe it's just not working but the person feeling that way is afraid to say so. The fact is, though, that not every relationship will go well. Honest communication and a willingness to either find answers or move on are needed.

Despite those potential pitfalls, as we close our discussion on mentors, my simple advice is to have them. Get past any embarrassment you might have over making yourself vulnerable to another person in this way. We men are typically reluctant to have these types of deep relationships. But the Bible encourages:

> Do not rebuke a mocker or he will hate you; rebuke a wise man and he will love you. Instruct a wise man and he will be wiser still; teach a righteous man and he will add to his learning. (Prov. 9:8-9)

If my own life and the many I've encouraged in this area are any indication, you'll find immense benefit from weaving your life together with those of your Timothy, Barnabas, and Paul, your "three strands." You will not be easily broken if you develop these relationships to support, help, and guide you. Hopefully this is an encouragement and starting point to your "three strands," and you can find further insight in some other valuable materials.[6]

Chapter 6 Q&A

1. How might one go about finding a mentor?

2. What do you think about having more than one mentor? How many mentors should one have?

3. How can you mentor team members at work or employees that report to you?

CHAPTER 7

Clear Witness

One time shortly after my promotion to vice president at Intel, I took a business trip that had me flying cross country. I found myself sitting next to a woman I hadn't met before, and we got to chatting. When she asked about my work and I described some of my recent successes, she seemed impressed.

When I reciprocated and asked about her work, she explained that she was the editor-in-chief for the parent company of our local Portland area newspaper and told me some of what that involved. After a bit, she asked what I thought of her paper.

Well, that local paper had earned a reputation for an anti-Christian bias, portraying Christians as unintelligent and weak in character. I took the opportunity to say politely that I found that bias not only personally offensive as a Christian, but also to be poor journalism and bad business practice.

The woman was surprised by my direct response, but to her credit and because I had previously established my credibility through my success at Intel, she took my concerns seriously. In a subsequent exchange of letters, she indicated her intent to address those concerns.

If you've made it this far and have begun implementing the first five principles I've suggested, you should be ready for this final piece—being a clear witness. If you've started making significant changes in your family, your work, and personal priorities, people will likely notice and say things like, "Hey, why are you leaving to go home at night earlier?" or "Why have you started not golfing with us on Sundays anymore?" or "I noticed you reading something the other day."

As these questions are thrown at you, how will you answer? Will you shyly deflect their interest with something like "It's nothing, just trying to improve myself a bit"? Or will you respectfully but truthfully declare your relationship with God and your conviction to living a more balanced life applying his principles?

> Whoever acknowledges me before men, I will also acknowledge him before my Father in heaven. But whoever disowns me before men, I will disown him before my Father in heaven. (Matt. 10:32-33)

This passage makes it clear that the answer to those seemingly minor or innocuous questions can have dramatic implications. Will we use them as springboards to share our lives and faith with another?

Far too often, we seem afraid or nervous to tell the truth. We'll duck the question or get embarrassed or tell a little lie (if there is such a thing). But let me challenge you to give the straightforward answer and be nothing but God's man or woman in those situations. When someone asks, "Why you don't golf on Sundays," respectfully and earnestly answer, "I've decided to prioritize my relationship with God, and I've committed to being in church. Further, I've decided I want my kids to see me being the spiritual leader of our household. I want to lead the way, and I want each of them to be learning from my example."

When you become a clear and visible witness, two powerful things happen. First, you've identified yourself publicly as a Christian. Second, you've just made yourself accountable to the people to whom you've identified yourself. Every time you are in that person's presence, you will now have to live up to a certain standard. As you become a clear witness to two, three, ten, twenty, or more individuals who see you at work, home, and play, all of a sudden you've developed a network of implied accountability.

In a short time, you will find you don't have any situations where you don't have some level of character accountability around you. This becomes a powerful tool to keep you on the right track. Once you've made it clear that you don't profane because of your position in Christ, for example, you can't be careless about it in the future because others are now ready to respond. I'm now well known for not drinking alcohol and have a network of many in the factory, in the field, and among our customers who keep me accountable to that standard.

Several years ago I was in a meeting with Andy Grove, and at one point he let loose a string of profanity to convey his dissatisfaction with something. His taking my Lord's name in vain didn't sit right with me, and I felt the Spirit compelling me to take action. Further, Andy is such a great man in so many regards that I felt he decreased his own image by resorting to such outbursts. Shortly thereafter, I decided I would speak to him.

With prayer and thoughtful preparation, I took him aside and said in the most respectful manner possible: "Andy, I would really appreciate it if you might avoid such profanities. I find them offensive and would just ask that you consider trying not to take my Lord's name in vain." What kind of crazy thing was I doing even suggesting such a thing? He's the big boss, a founder, president, board member. He can do whatever he likes, including firing me!

Well, to my surprise and delight, he responded receptively, saying, "You're right. Eva [Andy's wife] has been after me about this as well. I'll work on it."

Just a few weeks later I was at an Intel function that Eva also attended, and she purposely found me in the crowd. After greeting me, she quickly stated, "I've been after Andy for his profanity for many years. Thank you for calling him on this!" For many years after that, if Andy and I were in a meeting together and he slipped into profanity, he'd make eye contact knowingly, confirming that he recognized the slip, and reaffirming his accountability to me in this area.

I'm sure you'll find some hard core profaners who wouldn't respond with as much receptivity and dignity as Andy did, but I've had the same little talk with close to 100 people over the years, and every one of them has given me at least a respectful response. I don't attack their character or habit, just phrase my request in a most courteous manner.

A few years ago at Intel, a policy was instituted establishing employee support groups. The first of these was Globe, the Gay and Lesbian support group. While many were upset by the existence of such an entity, a few saw an opportunity to take advantage of the same policy and create the Intel Bible Christian Network, IBCN.

As they were getting IBCN off the ground, they desired to have a public and visible kick-off event. I was asked to speak. I was concerned that this was too visible a role for an executive to take. I also felt that if I did agree to speak, I needed to give an accurate and complete account of my Christian faith. After pondering, praying, and consulting a few others, I agreed to speak. To several audiences of several hundred each, I gave the first talk on "Juggling God, Family, and Work, Work, Work."

The speech was well received and led to a second, third, and fourth delivery of "Juggling" at other IBCN events. All of a sudden, I was exposing my Christian beliefs to hundreds of people inside the company.

As a result, many people got actively involved with IBCN. Several others were encouraged to be more open about their own faith. The most beneficial result, though, was that several other senior individuals in the company began stepping forward to identify themselves publicly as Christians. Being a clear witness was not only contagious, but in this case multiplicative as well.

Intel, like many employers, has also been an active supporter of United Way. As part of our Quarterly Business Update Meetings, United Way representatives would come in and give their short pitch, show a video, and ask for donations. Well, one recent year the United Way stood accused of a variety of inappropriate actions. Claims of impropriety were on the front pages of every newspaper. To add fuel to the controversy, United Way also decided to no longer support the Boy Scouts of America. The Boy Scouts had insisted on not having gay scout leaders, which raised great cries of protest from the gay community.

In the face of all that, Intel continued to support United Way. However, I couldn't bring myself to play even a passive role on behalf of the United Way fund raising campaign that year. I decided that United Way representatives would not participate in my group's Quarterly Business Update Meetings that cycle.

At this point, I was a general manager but not yet a VP or an executive staff member. As my position became known, my phone started to ring. Calls came from a VP in Oregon, then from another VP, next from the Oregon head of the United Way, and finally from the Chairman of Intel, Gordon Moore, who was personally chairing Intel's United Way campaign.

I held my ground. During the business update meetings, I gave my most impassioned plea to my hundreds of staffers to support local charities. I challenged each person to choose to make a huge difference. I did so, however, without mentioning the name of any specific charity.

I firmly believe that if you've implemented the other steps I've suggested in this book, you can be an effective and clear witness. For instance, if you've implemented the principles in chapter 5 and work hard, you have established your credibility and worth to your employer. Given this reputation and track record, your Invisible Value Account carries a high balance and you will be able to take a few deductions if required in specific character and priority testing situations like this one.

Many years ago when I was a junior engineer working on a portion of the 80386 design, another very senior engineer named Ed was working on another part of the chip. He was an avowed and vocal atheist. As we came to know of each other's strong views, Ed began to take me on as his personal target of assault. It was as if Ed were trying to revitalize the ancient Roman persecution of the Christians in the coliseum, and I was the main event. He became increasingly extreme in his private and public attacks on me.

Never being one to be quiet when attacked, I began sending him daily Scripture and devotionals on E-mail in response to each of his assertions. But my Scriptural proofs seemed to incite him all the more.

As this episode escalated and became increasingly public, an amazing thing occurred. Others of faith in the department, without encouragement or coaxing, began to stand up on my behalf. All of a sudden, people in restrooms and hallways would tell me that Ed was getting carried away, and they would describe their own beliefs and encourage me to remain strong in the face of these attacks.

While this experience was a far cry from the martyrdom of the first, second, and third centuries, or that which occurs today in some countries taking violent stands against Christians, I was left with a fresh perspective on how persecution is good for the individual and also for the community of believers. When lax and comfortable, our faith will wax, wane, and wobble. When confronted, we must make a clear decision to respond or ignore. In this particular example, none of this could have occurred if I was unwilling to be a visible witness. (By the way, while Ed came to have some respect for me, he never became a Christian to my knowledge, and I've lost track of him.)

Now, as a senior person for the company, I'm often called upon to represent Intel, and I regularly find my values tested in peculiar ways. Intel is a great company and runs ongoing training programs to remain ethical and consistent with our stated values and policies. As the company has progressed and gone through certain difficult issues like the Pentium flaw experience, our firm ethical stance has become more clear and sharp.

In 1998, we had a situation with a customer called Intergraph. I was one of the principal senior managers involved from Intel. Unfortunately, the situation went from bad to worse, and Intergraph eventually filed a lawsuit against Intel for contractual violations, intellectual property infringement, and violation of antitrust laws. Mine was one of the few names from Intel specifically mentioned in the lawsuit.

You can only imagine the depth of introspection this case caused me. How often I replayed the various meetings with Intergraph executives in my mind. Had I acted ethically? Had I done everything in my power to avoid this situation? What might I have done differently?

As the lawsuit proceeded, a reporter with *The Wall Street Journal* interviewed me one day on a variety of topics. At one point he blurted out, "Since you are a Christian, Pat, I think yours will be the most interesting testimony of them all in the Intergraph lawsuit."

I'd had no idea that Dean, the reporter, knew I was a Christian. But apparently, while he expected other Intel employees to tow the company line, he expected me as a Christian to tell the truth.

Well, the next day my Christian faith was being noted in the bible of the U.S. businessman, *The Wall Street Journal*. On the one hand, I was pleased to see my Christian faith noted publicly. However, to assert that it would lead me to confess things that non-Christians at Intel would not say was very troubling. Worse yet, some of the comments were taken by senior management in a very negative way. They felt I had given the impression that Christian employees like myself were more ethical than non-Christians. As this example showed me, being a clear witness is not without its risks. But it's what we are called to be as men and women of faith.

Looking for Help

I find that applying the principles in this book will create a reputation that will lead others to you in times of need. The husband of an administrative assistant in another department had cancer. The woman, whom I had not known previously, sought me out to let me know of the situation and ask for my prayers.

A coworker's girlfriend suddenly died. In our next conversation, the man told me how my witness over the years had been an encouragement to him in his recent ordeal.

I recently received mail from a man, Carl, who worked for me over ten years ago. He commented on how my witness was an on-going challenge to him. For many years, I haunted his thoughts and image of what a Christian was. Finally, many years after he had moved on from my organization, he became a Christian, citing my witness as a major influence in his life.

Imagine a conversation with a coworker in a time of medical or personal difficulty. You say, in the humblest and most empathetic of ways, "I'll be thinking of you and praying for you." Who, regardless of their faith, would not be encouraged by such a statement?

Of course, the soundest reason of them all to be a clear witness is from Scripture itself:

> You are the light of the world. A city on a hill cannot be hidden. Neither do people light a lamp and put it under a bowl. Instead they put it on its stand, and it gives light to everyone in the house. In the same way, let your light shine before men, that they may see your good deeds and praise your Father in heaven. (Matt. 5:14-16)

Let me reiterate at this point that your job is the place where you are to be a great employee. Your desire to be a witness should not supercede the performance of your duties and responsibilities. You must first become and then continue to be a great employee. Only then and when circumstances arise that don't interfere with your work can you have an effective witness.

Some Christians spend so much time witnessing at work that they cease to be great employees. That's wrong, and it will erode their position and reputation as employees. That, in turn, will hinder their credibility as witnesses. As with just about everything in this book, and most things in life, proper balance is the key.

I've had the opportunity to give this speech in a variety of situations while traveling with my job. While I'm in distant cities, Campus Crusade for Christ has been able to arrange speaking engagements where I can give my testimony or my juggling speech to business men and women, Christian groups, and men's meetings. I've enjoyed delivering this message, and I've even dusted off my juggling skills and used them as an object lesson. But while I enjoy the opportunities to speak, I only agree to them when they can be squeezed into my work schedule.

Intel does not fly me halfway around the world to be a wandering evangelist. They have me travel to get a job done, and I always challenge the Intel teams in the countries I visit to keep me entirely busy. With Intel employees worldwide I want to earn a reputation as a man who works hard for Intel. However, as weekends or evenings might be open, I take the opportunities to again be a clear witness.

At one particular Campus Crusade event in India, a senior and well-known press person asked to interview me about my talk. I considered this a great opportunity and agreed. However, when the conversation became a discussion of Intel business, it became important to clarify my two distinct roles. I was speaking at this venue as an individual, not as an Intel executive. To discuss Intel business, we would have to use Intel's normal press channels.

To be an effective witness in the workplace, you will need to learn and implement a clear separation of your position as a great employee (chapter 5) and clear witness (chapter 7). In the example I gave earlier about the Intergraph case and *The Wall Street Journal*, it was a learning experience for me. While I felt comfortable with my answers in the interview itself, seeing the reaction and how they came out in the press has led me to be much more precise about the clear separation between these two roles.

Finally, being a clear witness will require you to keep your own skills sharp as a person of faith.

> Preach the Word; be prepared in season and out of season; correct, rebuke and encourage—with great patience and careful instruction. (2 Tim. 4:2)

On one particular trip, the coworker I was traveling with was an atheist and was eager to challenge my clear witness with his own knowledge of the areas in the Bible that are hard to defend from a scientific perspective. By the time our flight was over, not only was our debate known to the entire business class of the flight we were on that day, but I was also challenged to study some of the many points he had made.

It turned out that this man had been an officer in a local organization of atheists. Despite that debate, however, we had a cordial working relationship over the ensuing years, until he retired from Intel. It doesn't appear as though he'll ever embrace Christianity, but I know he has heard the Gospel at least once.

As we've considered the five key principles in this book, I trust that you can now see how applying them will build up your reputation and influence in the workplace, in your home, in your church, and in your community. You will be seen as a man or woman of character and proper priorities. And that standing will afford you numerous opportunities to be a clear and bold witness for Jesus Christ.

Chapter 7 Q&A

1. How can you take opportunities to share God's Word at work? How would you do so? Are there any specific examples where you've been able to do so?

2. Under what circumstances would it be inappropriate to be a witness at your job?

3. What are some practical suggestions for being a witness at your job?

4. If one is not a Christian, can he or she still go about bringing balance to life?

CHAPTER 8

Power Juggling

After reading to this point, you might be tempted to think I've got it all together as a juggler of life's demands. Wrong! I didn't write this book because I'm perfect. Rather, writing it has reminded me of how much work I still have to do to juggle my duties and priorities properly.

As Linda and my own score sheet remind me, I'm working and traveling too much these days. Time for God and time for family are again in short supply. I don't need your admiration; I need your prayers. Like the apostle Paul in Philippians 3:14, I want to press on toward the prize God offers for faithfulness to his calling. And like you, I find that a constant struggle.

God is still teaching me, and I'm still learning. I hope that's true of you as well.

The chapters of this book have been presented in what I believe is the right order for working through them in your life.

Set a Course

Personal Mission—Begin by establishing a game plan for what you want your values to be, your personal mission statement. Decide what you want to accomplish in your life, and start setting a course that gets you there. We have so little of this precious resource called time and once you have spent it, you cannot get any of it back. Use it only in a manner consistent with your values and goals.

Your Highest Value

Prioritize God—Create a unique relationship between yourself and God that is consistently reinforced by your use of time. Create patterns and reminders in your life to help you remain in consistent dialogue and relationship with him. Be a visible and committed member of your place of worship. Use all your resources and finances consistent with God as your first priority.

Firmly Establish Your Second Highest Value

Prioritize Family—Establish your schedule so that other things do not squeeze out precious family time. Date your spouse. Spend individual time with each of your children. Put clear boundaries in place between work and family time. Be flexible, but when a season of work becomes prominent, make sure to take a period of focused time with your family to restore that proper balance.

Have Both God and Family in Proper Order

Work Hard—Be a great employee. Realize that ultimately you are not working for your boss, your president, or your company. Instead, you are working for God. In the end, his "well done" is the only reward that really matters. With the goal of heaven in view, look past anything that might distract you from being a great employee.

Keep True to Your Mission Statement

Develop a set of mentors—Create a network of individuals who keep you on track. Find one or two people you trust, respect, and are good in the areas that you are week in to be mentors to your personal and professional life. Look for both peers to keep you accountable and mentorees who could benefit from your experience.

Have a Clear Witness

Having developed a balanced life, with God, family, and work as your priorities, you will also develop a reputation as a great employee. That is when you are in position to be a clear witness for God at your job. You will have developed the credibility to influence others.

Returning to the image of a juggler, you're still trying to keep in the air a tennis ball for God, a soccer ball for work, and an odd-shaped football for your family (with teens). These six principles haven't changed the number or shape of the balls or how fast you need to handle them to keep them from falling. However, I hope they've given you some skills that can be applied consistently to the juggling task. Perhaps now you can begin to drop them less often, decrease the size of a few, and consciously decide when and if you should add another ball consistent with your long term mission.

Applying these six principles day in and day out is not easy. As I mentioned before, this is a journey. I'm still learning much in the process myself. I still fail in living by these priorities, and while I offer my Personal Mission Statement as a model for your own, I have a long way to go in accomplishing my goals.

Life today moves at an incredible speed. Don't be so foolish as to believe that after the next project or after the next assignment or when summer comes, you'll somehow get your family back on track and so on. I've heard it said that one definition of insanity is doing the same thing over and over and expecting different results. Things will not miraculously improve. You need to make some conscious decisions and tradeoffs.

My prayer and desire for you is that some of the principles and examples in this book will help you to master your priorities and make the right tradeoffs. May God's love and mercy surround you and his Holy Spirit fill you as you progress in your journey. Tomorrow, when you arise to begin your day of juggling, may you be purpose filled and deliberate in your desires, decisions, and directions. To waste time is a great evil; to use it wisely is the greatest blessing of a master juggler.

Responses to Q&As

Chapter 1

1. Many people would argue that the Internet is evil. What do you believe about it and other technologies that have been used in questionable manners?

   I believe that the Internet, like most everything in this world, can be used for good and, sadly, for evil as well. I'm personally excited about the enormous ministry potentials for the Net. For instance, we can use it to give the finest training and teaching to new church leaders everywhere on the globe. Maybe this tool will play a vital role in reaching all people groups for Christ.

2. The founder of Xerox, Chester Carlson, attributed his sustenance during difficult times to the 'Geeta,' the Hindu spiritual text. Don't you think that being spiritual is more important, whether you are a Christian, Hindu, or Muslim?

   There's great value in each of the major religions. While I've not studied each of them in depth, I find there is a great deal of commonality in the morality and ethics they each teach. I expect serious students and participants in any of them will lead more fulfilled lives and powerful personal and professional careers as a result. As I've met and become acquainted or even have gained close friends with people from many religions, I'd offer first-hand evidence that this is the case.

At the same time, I make no apologies for my personal faith in Christ Jesus and him alone. I believe Christianity to be unique. I believe Christ is the singular way to heaven (Acts 4:12) and it is Christ's death on the Cross by which every human being is offered a path to heaven. We are all sinners (Rom. 3:23). We all deserved eternal death (Rom. 6:23). We are uniquely saved by grace (Rom. 3:24) through Christ's blood (Eph. 2:13, 1 Pet. 1:18-19). If we have faith in him (Rom. 10:13), repent of our sins and are baptized into him (Acts 2:38) we will receive his Holy Spirit (Acts 2:38) and eternal life (Rom. 6:23).

While I respect that many who read this may be of Hindu or Muslim or other faiths, I could only pray that you would consider thoughtfully the unique claims of Christ as Savior and Lord. You can't consider him a great prophet or teacher and then ignore what he said. He claimed himself the Son of God, and he was either crazy or who he said he was.

3. In your time with God, do you ask God for help with your work or profession? Does God provide ideas, witty inventions, or specific help in the workplace? Do you have some ways to know what way to proceed, what direction to take in your work?

    Yes, we should be in constant communication with God in all areas of our lives (Phil. 4:6). I recall an instance when I asked my Bible study group for prayers for a difficult exam I was facing. A man of the church chided me about my request. He felt it was inappropriate to bring such trivial matters before God, particularly if I had properly studied for the exam. I disagreed with him at the time and strongly disagree today. We should bring all the requests and concerns of our daily lives before God. I've taken every major chip, project, organization, business or technology I've worked on for over twenty years at Intel before the throne of God. I suggest you do so with your work as well.

4. How does the average person cope with commitments to God and family compared to others who are far more capable or

talented? Don't average people need to work even harder to be great employees, making achieving balance impossible for the average person?

All biblical principles apply to all people regardless of their intelligence level, race, sex, skill, or role they are in. "Brilliant" people don't have fewer demands on them. In fact, the opposite is often true—the more gifted you are, the more opportunities you are provided to use those gifts. I'd point to Matthew 25 as a teaching of Jesus that confirms this point, or again in Luke 12:48. "From everyone who has been given much, much will be demanded; and from the one who has been entrusted with much, much more will be asked."

As a gifted person, you will have increased demands placed upon you to produce fruit. Also, the picture of the parable of the master and talents communicates that as you succeed with what talents you have, God will provide you with greater opportunities.

Each of us should be looking for ways and roles where our unique gifts can be used by God. Balancing our time becomes more of a challenge the more we do that. Thus, the principles and guidelines in this book apply to all people who are being challenged with balance in the workplace.

5. How do you know if you are in the right profession? Could the struggle with balance be because you are doing the wrong thing?

   Knowing the will of God for your life is a difficult challenge for anyone. I'd point to:

   Do not conform any longer to the pattern of this world, but be transformed by the renewing of your mind. Then you will be able to test and approve what God's will is—his good, pleasing and perfect will. (Romans 12:2)

   Clearly and consistently pursuing Christ will open up an understanding of your gifts and how you can be used by him. At some point, a job or career change may be appropriate.

Often, just learning to make him Lord and working for him as we discussed in Chapter 5 will make your current role far more fulfilling and satisfying. Soon after I became a Christian I felt compelled to leave technology and go into the ministry. I struggled with this for many months. I finally "laid a fleece before God" as Gideon had done in Judges 6 when he was seeking the Lord's direction. My fleece has remained dry to this day, and I consider this a clear answer from God that my ministry wasn't in leaving the work place and career I was in. Since then I've grown to see how God can use my current profession and role in mighty ways for his kingdom. As such, I'm confident I'm exactly where God wants me to be—at least for now.

Chapter 2

1. Why do you really need to prepare a Personal Mission Statement with specific values and goals?

   If you haven't yet, please do. If you've taken the time to get this far into the book, it is a must-do. As we've tried to develop through this chapter, a mission statement is a starting point to set a long-term direction for your life. What do you want to do with what you have left of your gift of time from God. What legacy will you leave on earth? It's like a compass for the decision we need to make every day.

2. What kind of time management tools do you use?

   You can find a variety of time management tools and systems. Some are computer based, and some attempt to integrate both priorities and goals as well as time management. Over the years I've used many with varying success. At different points in my professional career, different tools have been more or less appropriate.

   Generally, my simple conclusion is that it doesn't matter which you use or how you use them. The important point is having a Personal Mission Statement, periodically assessing your time, and putting in place some mechanisms to keep you living consistently with your goals. After you have your mis-

sion statement developed and in place, it is pretty easy to integrate the priorities that you have into any of the time-management tools available to you today.

3. How does one set goals or mission statements when the world around us changes so fast?

    Of course, your Personal Mission Statement will change over time, and you should periodically update and refine yours. However, as you try to write your mission statement, make the goals longer term and not too specific to an individual assignment or role. After completing mine about seven years ago, I've only needed to make minor modifications since.

4. How should one go about developing a will and detailed financial plan for his or her family?

    People often do these as they consider their life and plan more seriously. It isn't morbid to consider what happens when you die; it's prudent to plan for your family. Depending on the complexity of your estate and finances, you might be able to do these on your own with books or PC software that are now readily available. If your situation is more complicated, you may need to hire professionals such as a lawyer and financial planner. You will probably also want to update these every five to ten years to reflect your changing circumstances. Linda and I just updated our wills that we had developed about seven years ago.

Chapter 3

1. How can you make and keep God your number one priority in life?

    It is intensely difficult to put and then keep God on the throne of our lives in the face of so many activities, demands, and priorities. Having daily devotions, staying active in the local church, and letting mentors keep you accountable are some steps in the right direction.

2. Do you find your religious regimen ever getting to the point where it is little more than a daily routine? How can you put more of yourself into your personal devotions and prayer?

Yes, daily devotions can become routine. There are great resource materials to help us, however. The Necessity of Prayer by E. M. Bounds is maybe the greatest reference on the subject. Here are other ideas I've found useful:

- *Position—I cannot pray sitting for very long; I daydream or sleep. I can pray standing or on my knees.*

- *I am much more effective praying aloud than silently. Silently, my mind tends to wander. Aloud, it seems more personal and focused. I often pray when I'm driving, and if I do so out loud it can be an especially effective time of communication with God*

- *I follow the simple ACTS outline: Adoration or Acknowledge God (e.g., praise him, thank him), Confess my sins (be specific and thorough), Thanksgiving (Christ, Family, his provision, etc.) and finally Supplication (your list of requests, needs, and areas for his intervention).*

- *I find it useful to hum or sing praise songs as I pray, particularly when I'm in the "Acknowledge or Adoration" portion. Singing tends to take me into his presence and keep me there. Pray a while, sing a song, pray some more, sing again, pray again. Using Scripture directly in your prayers is powerful as well.*

- *Pray frequently. What I've outlined above is my once-a-day major time in devotions. However, often I find the greatest prayers to be those quick, spur of the moment prayers. Pray when you are walking into a meeting, when you are driving to work, when you see a need, and when you don't know what to say in a particular situation. (Phil. 4:6).*

3. Is it wise for someone who travels heavily or puts in late nights at work to commit to leading a weekly Bible study?

How can you fit your home Bible study into an already taxing schedule?

Prioritizing church activities is part of your commitment to God. Your work schedule may require those activities to occur on weekends. However, depending on your job requirements, having a home study may or may not be a good decision. Maybe leading a class on Sundays or a study on weekends or at lunchtime at the workplace would be more suitable.

In my case, I make an effort to be home on Wednesday evenings. However, due to business travel and other activities, I can't always make it. I have an individual, Ed, who works with me on the study and is ready to fill in for me whenever required.

4. How can you make your finances reflect God as the highest priority in your life?

Throughout the Old and New Testaments, we see a call to a life of giving to the Lord's work. As is the case with most laws and requirements of the Old Testament, they are replaced with loftier ideals and principles in the New Testament. The Bible has an awful lot to say about finances, which can't be ignored. Moving toward a life of Sacrifice, Blessing, Inheritance, and Agreement is a lifelong journey of financial stewardship that can be challenging but also extraordinarily rewarding both now and for eternity.

5. How do you deal with work assigned to you on a Sunday?

Two thoughts:

— Maybe some will disagree with me here, but I believe we are entirely under the new covenant. Thus, I don't believe we have a Sabbath law that we are required to obey. Throughout the New Testament we see Jesus at odds with the Pharisees over this exact point. However, the New Testament also calls for the consistent coming together in worship of believers. Thus, I wouldn't be too concerned about working on Sundays as long as you are in a worship service weekly. For

example, our church recently began a Saturday evening evangelistic service as an alternative for those who can't attend on Sundays.

— The Sabbath idea of time to rest and be focused on God remains valid and important, however. Preserving and enjoying such time is part of a healthy balance in one's life.

If you aren't able to consistently maintain balance and be in worship on a weekly basis, you should probably consider a different position where this can be the case.

Chapter 4

1. How do you prioritize your spouse above your children and profession?

   Both you and your spouse need to discuss this question thoughtfully. Explore where you might be letting the many demands of the kids or your job crowd your spouse out of his or her proper place in your life. What specific actions can you take to clearly communicate that your spouse, next to your relationship with God, is the most important relationship you have on this earth? There are some excellent resources available in your local Christian bookstore (check out Life Journey brand products, for instance).

2. Are regular dates with your spouse really that necessary? Why?

   This is a critical step in establishing your priorities. Through dating, weekends away, and focused communication on a regular basis, you can build an ongoing, ever deepening relationship with your spouse. When your children leave the home, you and your spouse will remain. Will you still know each other? Will you be more deeply in love with each other the day the last child leaves the nest than the day the two of you wed.

3. How can you make family time a priority in your regular weekly activities?

Some of the tools we've suggested, like one-on-one times during the week with each kid or a weekend checklist, will help. Find ways such as family vacations to create those memories that you and each member of your family will cherish for years to come. Invest the time in "family nights," in which everyone is required to not have any extra activities. The family has dinner together and spends the evening playing games and other activities together. (The Focus on the Family–Heritage Builder Family Nights Tool Chest products are a great resource for such.)

4. How does your spouse manage alone with the kids when you're away?

    Linda is a wonderful mother and tremendous support. Obviously she is blessed by God in her role as well. I also need to encourage her regularly and express my appreciation and gratitude. This is where things such as dating, gifts, cards, letters, and numerous other expressions of both love and gratitude are vital. I pray for her daily, too.

5. How would you handle a spouse who is intensely busy, gone a lot, not involved in church or family, and not responsive to your suggestions to alter his or her priorities?

    As with any situation, begin by taking the situation before God. Your job as a wife or husband is to be entirely supportive in all situations and for whatever length of time is required (Eph. 5:22-24; Col. 3:19, 1 Pet. 3:1-6). Your job as a husband is almost exactly parallel to that of the wife in each of these passages (Eph. 5:25-28, Col. 3:20-22, 1 Pet. 3:7). You can gently encourage your spouse to consider Scripture passages such as these; you might also ask him or her to read this book. If your mate is not a Christian, of course, your primary goal is to gently bring him or her to see Christ through both your lifestyle and your verbal witness (1 Pet. 3:1).

6. If your spouse is an extreme workaholic or simply refuses to adjust priorities, what can you do to improve the situation?

    Difficult situations like this seldom have easy answers.

Of course, continue to pray for your spouse to be open to change. With humility and an appealing spirit, continue to suggest change. While I have made adjustments over the years to my life and work balance, Linda's direct promptings, not random complaints or expressions of frustration, have often been the impetus for me to make changes. Since I'm still far from perfect, I am certain she will continue to encourage me to grow and improve my juggling skills.

You could also seek to discuss the situation with others whom your spouse respects and might listen to. Consider the possibility of counseling help as well.

As suggested by the answer to Question 2, you need always to remain supportive of your spouse, even in situations like this. This is easy to say but most difficult to do when your spouse is making obvious and painful mistakes, hurting your relationship and the family's. However, that is exactly what the Scriptures call you to do.

Finally, while you can't change your spouse, you can change yourself. Make sure you are correctly prioritizing your life and your relationship with your spouse even if he or she isn't yet doing so.

Chapter 5

1. How do you handle work commitments that come into conflict with family commitments?

   While I gave a few examples in the text, I have often put my family commitments above work demands. I am certain these conflicts will continue to arise, and I'm certain I will put family first many times.

   I would caution you not to be dogmatic about this in either direction. Sometimes a high priority work assignment will arise when you had a family commitment that was not particularly critical. Do your work assignment and do it well. Other times a modest work assignment will conflict with a family commitment; please honor the family commitment. Of course the difficult situations are when there's a high priority work assignment and a high priority family commitment. In these circumstances, keep the family commitment and be prepared for the potential consequences at work. Hopefully, by being a great employee, you will have established a strong balance in your invisible Value Account and can weather such situations with ease.

2. How can you manage when projects become intense and short target dates are set—when it becomes difficult to please family and friends while still being an effective employee?

The challenge of short target dates sometimes causes us to make choices that leave family time short. In the day and age of the Internet and mobile communications, demands come seven days a week, twenty-four hours a day. Many of our industries are global, making 24/7 a fact, not a phrase. Thus, these periods are to be expected and are often required. Make these tradeoffs and continue being a great employee. However, you must follow those intense work times with balancing times spent with family and friends.

Also, some jobs will turn into one intense period followed by another and another and so on. If these periods of intensity can never be balanced with family and God, you need to look at making more significant adjustments to your work and agenda, possibly even considering a new position in the company.

3. In an environment where corruption is a way to achieve goals, how can one maintain integrity?

There is no room for corruption in the Christian's life. As believers, we are constantly challenged by the Bible to live holy lives (2 Pet. 3:11). However, there is a fine line between doing your job as directed, aware that there may be corruption about you, and participating directly in corruption. It isn't your job or role to seek out corruption or questionable ethics. However, when you are confronted with ethic violations or corruption, you are obligated as a Christian to take appropriate steps to address it. Being a beacon of light in the midst of a corrupt world is what we are called to do as Christians (Matt. 5:13-16). This is where being a great employee, working hard, and yet living a moral and godly life can be the most powerful witness a Christian businessperson can have.

4. Would you continue to work hard even if you came across unethical behavior in your company?

   Absolutely. Remember that you work for God first and foremost (Col. 3:23). To make this point even more forcefully, look to 1 Peter 2:17, where Peter urges Christians to "honor the king." In Peter's day, the kings were none other than the evil Roman Caesars, who were persecuting the Christians and outlawing Christianity. Despite this extreme corruption, Peter urges respect and honor to the king who is in power only due to God's sovereign command. In fact, depending on the date of Peter's writing, the king at the time could have been Nero, who burned Christians at the stake to light his courts at night.

   Thus, the principle is powerful: work hard, as working for the Lord, despite the circumstances around you.

5. A bad economy puts a lot of pressure in our work lives. Where should one draw the line in terms of commitments and responsibilities?

   Times of pressure are when priorities and balance are more important than ever. We learn far more in difficult times or times of failure than we do in times of ease or success.

6. How do you see the trade-off between working to fill the pockets of another individual and earning a living for yourself?

   Work in its entirety is from God. We see this since the fall of man, when God ordained man to work to sustain life (Gen. 3:19). Not only was it instituted by God at this early time, but we see it consistently required through the Old Testament and the New as well (2 Thes. 3:10). Most of the great men and women of the Bible had professions before or in addition to their roles in ministry. Some worked independently (e.g., as shepherds or fishermen), others had bosses (e.g., tax collectors), and some were slaves (e.g., Philemon). But in all cases, the principles of work ethics seem to be asserted and applied (Col. 3:23).

Of course, some jobs seem inappropriate for Christians (bars, pornography, gambling). Thus, except for directly immoral positions, the key issue is not what kind of work you do or what kind of employer you have, but whether you're living a godly and holy life.

7. How often do you review your time chart?

    Typically I update it monthly and keep at least a year or more of history to see trends. Often, I have consistently difficult or busy periods of the year. Looking at a year helps me know these are coming up and work especially hard at being home either before or after.

Chapter 6

1. How might one go about finding a mentor?

    Carefully consider what areas you want to improve or grow in. Then look for people you trust and respect who are strong in those areas. Finally, make your desire known and ask for a commitment of adequate time. Also, seek out those for whom you might be a mentor. Develop relationships where you can be helping to mature others in both their professional and spiritual lives.

2. What do you think about having more than one mentor? How many mentors should one have?

    If you have a Paul, a Barnabas, and a Timothy in both your professional and spiritual lives, you would have six. If you had several ad hoc relationships as well, you might have a few more. Generally, I've never been able to maintain that many at one time and would advise you against trying to do so. I try to have one mentor/Paul, one I'm mentoring/Timothy, and one accountability partner/Barnabas. As long as I have those, I feel I've got that cord of three strands mentioned in Ecclesiastes.

Of course for some, just having one mentor is a big step forward. If you've never had any before, I'd strongly encourage you to start with just one mentor or peer as a starting point. After you've matured and developed in this way, you might be ready for a second.

3. How can you mentor team members at work or employees that report to you?

Mentoring is primarily a decision of the "mentoree" and not the mentor. And while encouraging those in your work family to seek and take such guidance, you cannot force it or require it. When I mentor people in my group, I take care not to show or even give the appearance of favoritism. I try to function as a coach to the individual, just as I would for most anyone on the team, and I encourage the person to find other mentors as well. Intel's open door policy helps, too; if any staff felt slighted, he or she could air a complaint to anyone above me in the chain of command.

Chapter 7

1. How can you take opportunities to share God's Word at work? How would you do so? Are there any specific examples where you've been able to do so?

   a. Your first witness in the workplace is being a great employee. If you don't do that, you will diminish any level of witness you might have.

   b. Your second witness is your lifestyle and ethics. Do you conduct your life with the highest of morals and ethics, or do you casually participate in corrupt or questionable behavior? Do you participate in crude discussions or joking? Do people see you having your personal devotions during your breaks and lunch hours?

c. *Third, you will get opportunities to express concern for others in a godly and genuine way. If a coworker is ill or has lost a family member, an "I'll be thinking of and praying for you," a gift of flowers, or a genuine "I'll come over and help you during your time of need" will speak volumes.*

d. *Finally, you may be afforded the occasional opportunity to witness verbally to others. This needs to be done with great prudence, lest you ever gain the reputation of using work time to proselytize others. This is also why I put such emphasis on being a "great employee" and putting your professional character above reproach. You must be even more cautious not to allow your position as a supervisor to place pressure on a subordinate in this regard. You should never witness during work time, only during breaks or off time.*

A specific example might be a recent instance where a coworker's girlfriend fell unexpectedly ill and quickly died. Given points 1-3 above, I had a great opportunity to talk with him about faith in Christ in a casual yet profound way.

2. Under what circumstances would it be inappropriate to be a witness at your job?

As suggested in the answer to the last question, you can always witness through your work and character. Expressing concern should be done as the occasions allow and as often as God brings them your way. I would suggest caution in being too bold with witnessing at your job until you've developed a balance in your value account. Also, be careful of any policies your company might have in this regard. As already covered, never let your desire to witness become a distraction to being a great employee. Finally, beware of witnessing during your normal work hours. It's a matter of Christian integrity and a living witness that those hours be focused on your work. Christians need to be above reproach in every regard.

3. What are some practical suggestions for being a witness at your job?

   Your attitude, more than anything else, will influence your effectiveness. If you approach others with humility, respect, and heart-felt concern, coworkers will generally give great deference to the message you have to offer.

   Also, being a clear witness is best done where a relationship already exists. First develop that relationship, and then build and expand to other areas of your life, including your faith.

   Being a witness is often done in trivial ways of what you say or how you react to a situation. Reacting in a godly way to a difficult circumstance might be the most powerful witness you'll ever have. For instance, I make it a point to carry a joyous demeanor even in difficult times. As people ask what I'm happy about, I can often share more of my life and faith.

4. If one is not a Christian, can he or she still go about bringing balance to life?

   I do believe that the only true balance one can find in life is through Christ. Nevertheless, most of the tools in these chapters can still be applied (as is the case with many Christian truths). Chapters 3 and 7 are pretty specific to Christians and those of faith. Even in those cases, though, most of the practical advice in the other chapters will still be useful. But consider this premise—if it is useful and true, consider the source.

Endnotes

[1] Buford, Bob, *Half Time,* Grand Rapids, Michigan: Zondervan Publishing, 1994

[2] Crawford, John and Patrick Gelsinger, *Programming the 80386,* Alameda, Calif.: Sybex 1987.

[3] Encyclopedia Britannica, 1999 Britannica Book of the Year.

[4] Alcorn, Randy, *The Treasure Principle*, Sisters, Oregon: Lifechange Books, 2001.

[5] McLaughlin, David, *The Role of the Man in the Family*, Neenah, Wisconsin: David McGlaughlin video series.

[6] Two sources recommended:
   • *Seven Promises of a Promise Keeper,* Chapter 2 "Promise 2 A Man and His Mentors," pg 47-67, Colorado Springs, Colorado: Focus on the Family Publishing, 1994
   • Hendricks, Howard and Hendricks, William, *As Iron Sharpens Iron*, Chicago, Illinois: Moody Press, 1995.